USEFUL MAXIMS

IN A WORLD OF EMPTY SPEAK

USEFUL MAXIMS

IN A WORLD OF EMPTY SPEAK

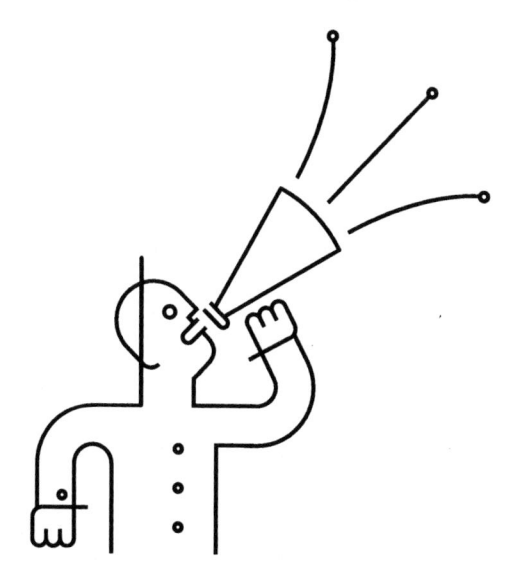

BRIAN RIDOLFI

AMBASSADOR INTERNATIONAL
GREENVILLE, SOUTH CAROLINA & BELFAST, NORTHERN IRELAND
www.ambassador-international.com

USEFUL MAXIMS
In A World of Empty Speak

© 2012 by Brian Ridolfi
All rights reserved

Printed in the United States of America

ISBN: 978-1-62020-002-5
eISBN: 978-1-62020-004-9

Unless otherwise indicated all Scripture quotations are taken from King James Version.

Cover Design and Page Layout by Matthew Mulder

AMBASSADOR INTERNATIONAL
Emerald House
427 Wade Hampton Blvd.
Greenville, SC 29609, USA
www.ambassador-international.com

AMBASSADOR BOOKS
The Mount
2 Woodstock Link
Belfast, BT6 8DD, Northern Ireland, UK
www.ambassador-international.com

The colophon is a trademark of Ambassador

To all the laborers of the harvest fighting the good fight.

Endorsements

"Our culture is short on wisdom, but this short book is not. Every page of *Useful Maxims* reveals time-tested truths from the Bible, philosophy and experience that will inform and entertain you, hopefully to a life better lived (but that last part is up to you). There are plenty of "ah-hah!" moments in here."

—Dr. Frank Turek, co author,
I Don't Have Enough Faith to be an Atheist

"The only thing better than speaking the truth is speaking the truth well. The epigrammatic Brian Ridolfi makes language not only his toy but his tool as he deals one provocative and memorable quote after another."

—Dale Ahlquist, President, American Chesterton Society

Table of Content

Preface 21

CHAPTER 1

God 23

God's Characteristics 23
God's Nature 24
God's Way 25
God's Presence 25
God's Existence 25
God's Salvation 25
God's People 26
God vs. Man 27
God's Power 28
God's Kingdom 28
Prayer 28
Divine Providence 28
God's Immutability 29
God's Law 29
God's Requirements 29
God's Justice and Judgment 29
God's Fidelity 29
God's Trials 29
Finding God 29

CHAPTER 2

Morality & The Human Condition. 31

Religiosity vs. Righteousness 31
Faith 32
Masters and Servants 32
Uprightness. 32
Stumbling Blocks. 33
Nominal Christianity 33
Worldly Christianity. 33
Moral Regression 33
Backsliding 33
Self-denial 33
Integrity 34
Waywardness 34
Falls 34
Narcissism 35
Sin 35
Purpose. 35
Defeat. 36
Self-discipline 36
Preferential Treatment. 36
Ignorance 36
Denominationalism 36
Commandments 36
God's Word 37
Holy Scripture. 37
The Fear of the Lord 37
Conscience 37
Repentance. 38
Self-improvement 38
New Man and Old Man. 38
Vision 38
Focus 39
Pantheism 39

Freedom	39
Promises	39
Hypocrisy	39
True Character	40
Indifference	40
Mission	40
Charity	40
Complicitness	41
Meekness	41
Achievement	41
Affirmation	42
Self-exaltation	42
Strength and Weakness	42
Ability	43
Stagnation	43
Adversity	44
Perfectionism	45
Compulsiveness	45
Self-control	45
Moral Standards	45
Cafeteria Morality	46
Atheism	46
Internal Conflict	47
Choices	47
Prudence	47
Depravity	47
Carelessness	48
Idleness	48
Addiction	48
Health	49
Feelings	49
Life and Death	50

CHAPTER 3

Relationships & Conflict 51
Inherent Strife. 51
Concord 52
Discord. 52
Ethnic Fighting 53
Equality. 53
Peacetakers 53
Peacemakers 53
Grudge 54
Spite 54
Revenge 54
Reconciliation. 54
Consideration 54
Self-centeredness 55
Deterrence 55
Trust 55
Honor. 55
Self-condemnation. 56
Justice 56
Exploit 56
Oppression 56
Disparity. 57
Longevity 57
Lack of Restraint 57
Infection 58
Child Rearing 58
Deterioration. 59
Bad Company 59
Difficulty and Complexity 60
War. 60
Firearms 60
Taking a Stand 60
Pacifism. 61

Rules of Engagement............................61
Methodology and Tactics..........................61
Peaceful Existences.............................. 62
Division...................................... 62
Volatility..................................... 63
Freedom of Conscience........................... 63
Incompatibility................................ 64
Refuge....................................... 64
Brutes.. 64
Turmoil....................................... 64
Unity... 65
Egalitarianism................................. 65
Political and Financial Instability...................... 65
Aggravation and Insecurity......................... 66
Survival of the Weakest............................ 66
Tolerance...................................... 66
Offense....................................... 67
Modern Multiculturalism.......................... 67
Inclusiveness.................................. 67
Permissiveness................................. 67
Admonition.................................... 68
Intercession................................... 68
Stubbornness.................................. 68
Pack Mentality.................................. 68
Worldly Persecution.............................. 69
Violent Resistance............................... 69
Haste.. 70
Foresight......................................71
Overload...................................... 72
Inability...................................... 72
Sameness..................................... 73
Indicators.................................... 73
Advancement................................... 73
Attraction and Infatuation.......................... 73
Lust.. 73
Objectification................................. 74

The Male/Female Relationship. 74
Harlotry 74
The Sexual Revolution 75
Destruction of the Family. 75

CHAPTER 4

Hearts & Minds 77

Noise 77
Overwhelming Concern 77
Wisdom. 78
Experience 78
Sight. 78
Questions and Answers. 79
Obstinacy 79
Discernment 79
Cheap Rhetoric. 79
Understanding. 80
Maturity 80
The Exchange of Ideas 80
Discourse 80
The Rise of Iniquity 80
Hostility Toward God. 81
Control. 81
Indulgence 81
Blindness. 81
Awareness 81
Lack of Knowledge 82
Lack of Concern 82
Christianity and Christians 83
Apostasy 83
The Bible 84
Preparedness 84
Details. 84
Collateral Damage 84

Words 85
Vetting 85
Multitude of Words 85
Few Words 86
Character Assassins 86
Light and Darkness 87
Truth 87
Lies and Liars 87
Fraud and Charlatans 88
Relativism and Existentialism 88
Utilitarianism 89
Secularism 89
Humanism 90
Futility 90
Fools 90
Robots 90
Spiteful Mouths 90
Loose Tongues 91
Flattery 91
Conditioning 91
Propaganda 91
Political Correctness 92
Volition 92
Faulty Information 92
Disbelief 92
Arguments 92
Education 93
Know-It-Alls 93
Elitism 93
Leniency 93
One-sidedness 93
Desensitization 94
Diversion 94
Stimulation 94
Amusement 94
Social Decay 94

Impulsiveness and Recklessness	95
Hedonism	95
Corrupted Cultures	95
Insipidness	95
The Mind	96
Good Sense	96
Common Sense	96
Soundness	96
Abandoned Logic	96
Foolishness in Charge	96
Entertainment	97
Convolution	97
Demagoguery	97
Influence	97
Service	98
The Great Commission	98
Help and Assistance	98
Admission of Fault	98
Zealotry and Extremism	98
Perception	99
Scales	99
Bias	99
Agendas	99
The Unseen Factor	99
Plots	100
Forgotten Threats	101
Technology	101
The Herd	101
Unhealthy Spirits	102
Completeness	102
Liberation	102
Dissatisfaction	102
Worry	103
Rest	103
Exhaustion	103
Healthy Minds	103

CHAPTER 5

Science & Philosophy 105
Existence. 105
Order and Complexity. 106
Singularity. 106
Rationalism. 106
Presupposition 107
Context. 107
Philosophy. 107
Naturalism. 107
Scientism. 108
Science and Religion. 108
Evolution 108
Uniformitarianism. 112
Uncertainty. 113
Chance 113
Forces 113
Space-Time Continuum. 113

CHAPTER 6

Evil, Suffering, & Judgment 115
Evil's Attributes 115
Evil Worlds 116
The Rise of Evil 116
Evil on the Run 117
Allowing Evil. 117
Evil's Presence 117
Man's Sinful Nature 117
Death 118
Suffering 118
How Evil Is Fought 118
The Devil and Devils 118

Systematic Evil 119
Pure and Impure Evil. 120
The Occult 120
False Religion 120
Evil Partaken. 121
Redefined Evil 121
Evildoers. 121
Judgment. 121
Salvation and Damnation 121
Heaven and Hell 122
Battling Evil 123

CHAPTER 7

Economics 125

Patience. 125
The Rush to Be Rich 126
Evaporation of Wealth 126
Avarice 126
Materialism 126
Consumerism 127
Vain Endeavors. 127
Gluttony 127
Gleaning 128
Prosperity 128
Work Ethic 129
Poor Management 129
Cheapness 129
Outsourcing 130
Purchasing Power. 130
Short-sidedness 130
Labor 130
Shaky Ground 130
Tried and True Practices 131
Efficiency 131

Groundwork 132
Consequence 132
Socialism 132
Economic Philosophy 132
Government Intervention 133
Economies 133
Economic Systems 134
Saving 134
Hedging 134
Planting 134
Money 135
Conservation 135
Yield 135
Easy Fortunes 136
Covetousness 136
Enterprise 136
Initiative 136
Contentment 137
Accumulation 137
Mortgages and Homes 138
Financing 138
Possessions 138
Value 138
Usury 139
Debt 139
Rich and Poor 140
Consumer Awareness 140

CHAPTER 8

Law, Government, and Civics 141
Loss of Liberty 141
Temperance 142
Big Government and Big Business 142
Communism 142

Checks and Balances 144
Lost Generations 144
The Silent Majority 144
Minority Rule. 145
Counterfeit Authority 145
Small but Dangerous Cabals 145
Unrestricted Restrictions 146
Neglect. 146
Eugenics 146
Subjugation. 147
Political Strife 147
Church and State 148
Civility 148
Breakdown of the Rule of Law. 148
Mob Tyranny. 149
Law's Foundation. 149
Unjust Balances 149
The Rule of Men 149
Corrupted Authority 149
Legislation from the Bench. 150
Lack of Justice 150
Poor Government 150
Power 150
Stable Government 151
Godly Disobedience. 151
Government's Responsibility 152
Ungodly Nations. 152
Rulers. 152
Political Slavery 153
Free Money. 154
Taxes. 154
Social Justice 155
Accountability 155
Self-reliance. 155
Individual Action. 155
Grassroots Insurgencies. 156

Domestication 156
Political Despair 156
Phony Politicians 156
The Democratic Process 157
Leadership 158
Polls 158
Infiltration 158
Defensive Action 159
Complacency 160
Duplicity 162
Middle Ground 162
Final Words 164

Notes 165
Section A: References 167
Section B: Glossary of Terms 211

Preface

Benjamin Franklin's *Poor Richard's Almanac*, published between 1732 and 1757, is a great example of sagely wisdom. Who can forget "an apple a day keeps the doctor away" or "a penny saved is a penny earned"? To this day Franklin's maxims remain a part of our common vernacular. But perhaps history's most notable sage was Solomon, the king of Israel who reigned between 970 and 930 B.C. He wrote his proverbs some three thousand years before Franklin was even born. His sayings include: "Curse not the king, no not in thy thought; and curse not the rich in thy bedchamber: for a bird of the air shall carry the voice, and that which hath wings shall tell the matter" (Ecclesiastes 10:20) and "Wilt thou set thine eyes upon that which is not? for riches certainly make themselves wings; they fly away as an eagle toward heaven" (Proverbs 23:5). Over the years others followed Solomon and Franklin with more adages, like G.K. Chesterton and C.S. Lewis. Now you are about to read some of my own axioms.

Sagacious wisdom is needed now maybe more than ever. The modern world is a hectic place; it is easy to get lost nowadays because information is everywhere, but little of it makes any sense. In situations like these, it is best to take a step back, breathe, and focus. Poignant sayings like the ones in this book are great for this very purpose. They get to the point quickly, unlike treatises, and they are memorable, not like dry dissertations. The things we remember most are the simplest things. Wisdom literature teaches in a way no other literary device can. Didactic proverbs are concise and easy to read. Summed up in one wise maxim can be an encyclopedia of information.

The wisdom contained in this book is not new; some of it might be familiar, and some of it may not, but all of it is either biblical in nature or common sense. So get ready and be prepared to gain insight on God, morality, conflict, subversion, science, philosophy, evil, economics, law, government, and other topics. Also, feel free to highlight sections you like. If I have done my job well, by the time you finish this book, the whole thing ought to be highlighted.

CHAPTER 1

God

God's Characteristics

Everyone is religious except God, for only God knows all the facts.

Only one thing about God: He is the only God.[1]

One truth about God: He is one.[2]

The difference between God and gods: God creates,[3] and gods are created.[4]

God's Nature

God cannot lie, it is against His nature;[5] the person who says God speaks with different voices calls God a liar.

Anyone who denies the *Trinity* calls God *schizophrenic*, for if the *Godhead* was not comprised of three separate individuals, why else would He say, "Let **us** make man in **our** image, after **our** likeness:"?[6]

God is not an idol, nor is He a man, or even an angel. God is a Spirit.[7] He is One divine being[2] who exists as three separate persons. There are not three gods but One God comprised of three individuals.[8] Each individual is congruous to the others; they lack nothing and share the same holy nature.

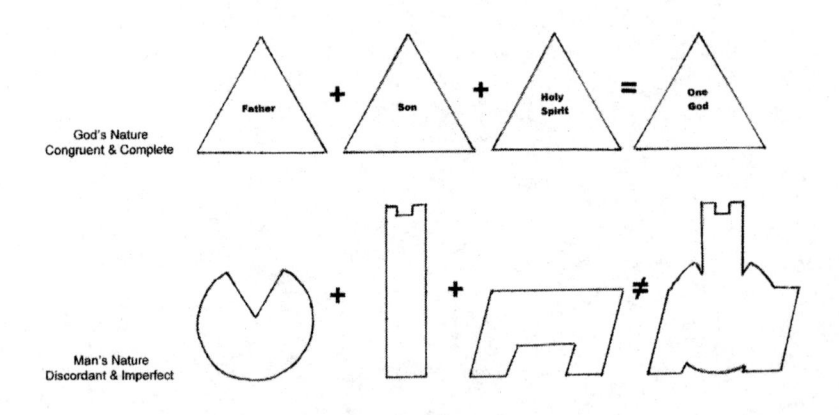

God's Nature
Congruent & Complete

△ Father + △ Son + △ Holy Spirit = △ One God

Man's Nature
Discordant & Imperfect

The first person of the *Godhead* is God the Father, the second is God the Son, and the third is God the Holy Spirit. God the Father is the source of everything. He sent Jesus Christ into the world to save it.[9] God the Son is the *WORD OF GOD*, the world and everything in it was created by Him and for Him.[10] He is the Savior and image of the Father.[11] When we see the Son, we see the Father.[12] God the Holy Spirit is the Spirit of truth and a witness. He dwells in the saved and proceeds from the Father and testifies of the Son.[13]

God never changes;[14] He always gets changed.[15]

God is slow to wrath, [16] but His wrath is quick. [17]

Jesus Christ is Lion as well as Lamb. [18]

God's Way

God works in seasons and for reasons.

God's ways are mysterious because we are unaware.

To reveal or to conceal is God's prerogative. [19]

God's Presence

Nobody sees God, but everybody sees manifestations of Him; nobody sees atoms either, but everybody sees what they make.

If you saw God, you would see you cannot stand before Him. [20]

You will not see the Father as He is until you see the Son for what He is.

God's Existence

The roof is proof God exists. [21]

Unlike *Nietzsche*, God is alive.

God created life; life did not create God.

Life exists because God exists.

God's Salvation

To speak to man, God became man. [22]

Jesus became like us so we could become like Him. [23]

Christ lowered Himself to our level [24] because we cannot raise ourselves to His.

Only a perfect *Redeemer* can purchase perfect redemption. [25]

Jesus Christ did what He said [26] and said what He did. [27]

Christ's body died on the cross so our souls would not die in the *Lake of Fire*.

The body lives long when it eats the right foods, and the soul lives forever when it eats the body of Christ. [28]

HE HAVING THE MOST FORCE is least forceful.

God does not impose His salvation on anyone.

It is not God's will to save anyone against their will.

God prefers persuasion over invasion.

Plentitude is friendship with God over servitude. [29]

Automatons automatically cannot please God.

God helps them who help themselves to His free gift of salvation.

To sin against the Holy Spirit is to sin against salvation. Christ was crucified only once; the moment we are sealed by the Holy Spirit we cannot be sealed again; Christ's sacrifice cannot be received twice. [30]

God's People

God did not replace the *Apple of His Eye* with the *Body of His Son*. [31]

God goes the extra mile; He uses both *Jew* and *Gentile*.

Some *Jews* are *Christian*, [32] all *Christians* are *Jews*, [33] and nobody for God is against God. [34]

That which He crafted, [35] God grafted. [36]

God ordained that from *Abraham* lawgivers would come, prophets, and kings, and ultimately The *Lawgiver*, The *Prophet*, and The *King of kings and Lord of lords*. Israel came from Abraham's covenant with God, [37] and The

Messiah came out of Israel.[38] *Abraham* fathered the nation that brought forth The *Messiah*, The *Branch of Jesse*, The *Root of David*, The One who would not only redeem Israel, but the entire world.

God vs. Man

God made man for His pleasure,[39] not pleasure for His man.

God made man in His own image, and man makes himself in his own imaginations.[40]

Do not apply man's limited human nature to God's limitless divine nature. God is infinite, and men are finite. To God, time is irrelevant; finite beings react in time, but God can act before and after time, outside of time, throughout time, at any time.[41]

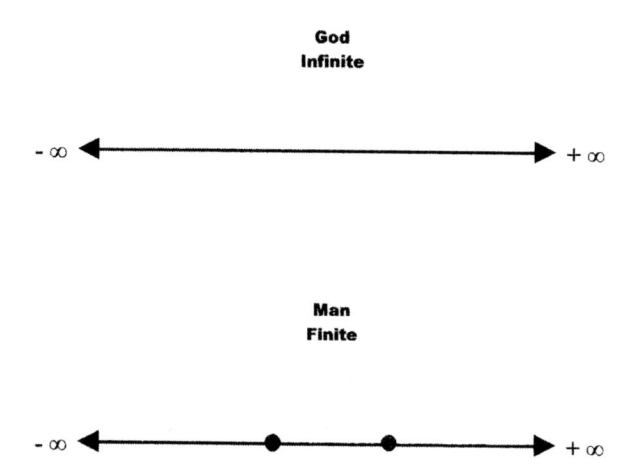

God
Infinite

$-\infty \longleftarrow \longrightarrow +\infty$

Man
Finite

$-\infty \longleftarrow \bullet \longrightarrow \bullet \longrightarrow +\infty$

God's Power

The only thing God cannot do is sin.[5]

God handles everything because everything is in His hand.[42]

God's Kingdom

Men do not dwell in the kingdom of God; the kingdom of God dwells in men.[43]

Prayer

Our tears enter God's ears.[44]

God always answers prayer, but He does not always grant petition.

Genies grant wishes; God grants favor.[45]

Namely, those who pray in God's name are named as recipients.[46]

God is able to give more than any man is able to ask.

Divine Providence

God is free to choose men who choose freedom.

Just wait; God is never late.

Divine Predestination is the way by which God brings men to their supreme destination.

If God gives you a mission, you will always be in the right position.

All the luck in the world cannot equal one speck of God's grace.

Divine Providence is more than providential.

God finds you before you find Him.[47]

Gods sows for the ones He knows.[48]

God's Immutability

If God never said it, He never spread it.

Anything not of God is not from God.

God's *immutability* gives Him the ability to speak with irrefutability.

God's Law

Commandments are not there to resist, but to assist. [49]

God says no to man because man says yes to sin.

God's Requirements

All God requires from man is man's all. [50]

God's Justice and Judgment

If God just did not judge sin, He would not be a just God.

God judges who remains judge. [51]

God's Fidelity

If you cleave, God will not leave.

God never leaves, He is always left.

God's Trials

To purify, the Lord proves. [52]

God never disjoints those joined with Him. [53]

Finding God

The searched for search for God. [54]

Losing oneself is the first step to finding God. [55]

Pride is bound before God is found.

The last to seek *Idols* are the first to see God.[56]

CHAPTER 2

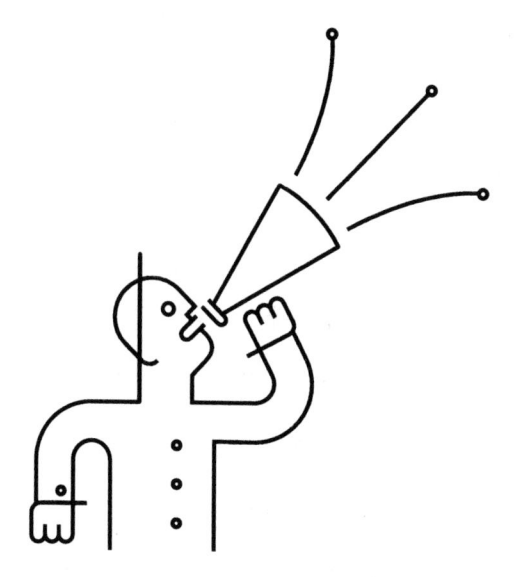

Morality & The Human Condition

Religiosity vs. Righteousness

A borne cross is better than a worn cross. [1]

Sporting crosses shows religiousness, and supporting them shows righteousness. [1]

Going to church is good; going to God is better.

Fill souls rather than *pews*.

Sacrifices are good intentions when they are intended for good.

Faith

Belief alone does not transform; belief must become faith, and faith, action. [2]

Faith without works, and works without faith, do not work out one's faith. [2]

No faith, no chance.

Those that abound in faith abound in grace. [3]

Masters and Servants

Choose a master, or one will be chosen for you.

If you do not bow before God, you will surely bow before men.

Who we serve determines what kind of people we are. [4]

The things that motivate also dominate.

Servants of everything are servants to anything.

Uprightness

The difference between the upright and the abased: upright men are on their knees before God, and abased men were on their feet before God cut them down. [5]

Those who look up to God are looked up to.

Righteousness is contagious.

Stumbling Blocks

Good men who do good are examples to others,[6] and good men who do evil are stumbling blocks for sinners.[7]

Satan's job becomes simple whenever *Christians* act like simpletons.

Nominal Christianity

Nominal *Christians* who love evil nominally are not *Christian*.

Dung in a beautiful package still smells like dung.

Worldly Christianity

You cannot overshadow the world if you dwell under its silhouette.

Salt which savors the world loses its savoriness.[8]

Indulgent *Christians* indulge in worldliness.

Moral Regression

Wretchedness lives where righteousness dies.

There can be no dissolute progress without moral regress.

The concerted get converted every time the perverted get asserted.

Backsliding

People turn back to *paganism* once they turn their backs to God.

Perverts revert back to evil.[9]

Backsliders and sidewinders slither themselves back into holes.

Self-denial

Righteousness takes effort; more pain now means less pain later.[10]

Sometimes to defend ourselves, we must offend ourselves.

Quite often the simplest decisions are the hardest ones we make.

Going against nature is naturally difficult.

Integrity

Net integrity is equal to the sum of the moral components minus the sum of the immoral components.

Waywardness

Being sleazy is easy—that is, until sleaziness becomes uneasiness.

Moving downhill is easier than moving uphill; likewise, being bad is simpler than being good.

As *entropy* is the law of nature, *moral entropy* is the law of human nature.

Immorality in motion will continue in motion unless it experiences a net godly force.

Men fray before they stray.

There are only two types of people: those advancing toward salvation, and those retreating from light into darkness away from emancipation.

Progress is not good if you are progressing in the wrong direction.

If you are not anchored to the *Rock*, you will drift out to sea, and it is hard to find your way back after you waft too far.

Falls

God does not push people over; people pull themselves under.

Hands that do not reach for God cannot be reached by God.

God always seeks the fallen,[11] but the fallen never seek God.[12]

When the Spirit is not there to stop a fall, the fall is endless.

Depravity lets in when gravity sets in.

Narcissism

Narcissists and cancer cysts *metastasize*.

A diseased man wanted to join a crowd. He knew he was contagious and could contaminate others, but he did not care because his only concern was himself. One day the crowd allowed him to enlist, and unbeknownst to them, he was infectious. Over time the group became very ill, and some even died, but the diseased man was not moved by their suffering.

This is the explanation of the parable: the diseased man represents narcissistic sinners, and the group represents society.

Narcissists bring society down, and they are not even interested. As long as they get what they want, they could not care less about others. They know their sins are harmful, but instead of repenting, they prefer spreading sin around and tainting others with it until everyone is just as miserable as they are.

Sin

Sin is like cancer; once it takes over, removing all traces of it can be just as painful as the disease itself.

Sin starts with pride [13] and ends in death. [14]

Purpose

Getting to the goal is the only goal in life.

Man's duty is dutifully expressed in the Bible. [15]

When God is nowhere to be seen, human beings no longer see their purpose.

Defeat

We fail when we faint.[16]

The battle is through when the towel is thrown, and the war is done when there is nowhere to run.

One loses when one loses one's soul.

Better to be defeated by a tough opponent than by an easy mistake.

Self-discipline

Because man cannot keep himself, he cannot keep the law himself.[17]

Preferential Treatment

Good demeanor does not validate bad behavior.

Pleasant people do some very unpleasant things.

Actions—not conditions—ought to activate decisions.

Ignorance

Those who forget God beget fraud.

Deaf ears cannot hear, and dead spirits do not understand.[18]

The simple ignore God's simple message.

Denominationalism

There are many *Christian* denominations because there are many *Christian* interpretations.

Commandments

Broken commandments break down integrity.

Morality & The Human Condition

The Ten Commandments [19] teach what is sin, and the Great Commandment makes fulfilling the Ten Commandments possible. [20]

God's Word

Whenever heeded, God's word is seeded, [21] and whenever taken lightly, it is taken away. [22]

Holy Scripture

There is nothing new about the *New Testament* [23] and nothing old about the *Old Testament*. [24]

The Bible's meaning is not hidden from men; [25] men hide from its meaning. [26]

Seek Scriptures when you seek answers.

Scripture is a referee as well as a reference.

All Scripture is reliable because it all comes from a reliable God. [27]

The Bible is its own *Rosetta Stone*.

The Fear of the Lord

Exercise strengthens the body, and learning enhances the mind; the fear of the Lord bolsters the spirit. [28]

If you fear God, you do not need to fear anything else. [29]

Conscience

Everyone understands right and wrong; because of that, no one has an excuse for sin. [30] God's commandments dwell inside our hearts; [31] we sin either because we ignore our conscience or because our conscience is weak.

Everyone is a slave. Slaves to sin cannot endure temptation because it is irresistible, and slaves to righteousness cannot live in sin because their conscience vexes them, or because transgression tastes bitter in their mouths.

Every seared conscience sears everything.

Repentance

The difference between saints and sinners: a sinner sins without remorse, and a saint sins, but he repents with a contrite heart.

Better to repent than to lament.

Self-improvement

Unless a man gains victory over himself, he himself will never gain victory.

If you want to make the world a better place, start by making yourself a better man.

Try conquering yourself before you try conquering the world.

If you want to see your biggest enemy, look in the mirror.

New Man and Old Man

The new man can defeat the old man;[32] if you want to overcome yourself, stand beside yourself.

You cannot change what you are until you change who you are.

A different Spirit makes all the difference in the world.[33]

Rebirth is spiritual birth.[34]

Vision

Spoiled souls and soiled panes obstruct vision.

Where the eye looks, the mind will follow; look beyond today, and you will have a better tomorrow.

Focus

Focused eyes are never distracted, and a one-track mind is on the right track when it minds no folly.

The right resolve gets you the right result.

The determined are determined to succeed.

Pantheism

Wide worldviews widen danger. [35]

Freedom

It is one hundred percent true that we are not one hundred percent free. Because we are free to act does not mean we are free from the consequences of our actions.

Free men are free to enslave themselves.

Free men begin as slaves. [36]

Remaining free is harder than gaining freedom.

Promises

If you cannot deliver, do not deliver lip service.

Vow breakers are avowed fakers.

Hypocrisy

If you cannot teach with moral clarity, do not preach with your oral cavity.

Do not stand on moral high ground if it does not support you. Actions are better indicators of character than rhetoric; unless words are backed up by deeds, they are only words.

A moral teaching from an immoral teacher is like an awful leaching from a liberal fissure.

True Character

Makeup makes up character.

True nature is revealed by natural action.[37]

From time to time the lid comes off one's *Id*.

Indifference

The indifferent make no difference.

Mission

If the wrong person is in command, the right mission will fail before anyone can lay a hand.

Godly mission begins with submission.

Charity

It is all true: *Altruism* is all good.

The helped go on to help.

He helps himself who helps others.

Give smart; do not just give.

Righteous charities do more good with a little than evil charities do with a lot.

Usable amount matters more than amount used.

What is able beats what is on the table.

Bearing fruit is more important than sharing loot.

Righteous men who donate to evil causes are like lambs that births lions.

Complicitness

To support an evildoer is to be complicit with an evildoer.

Those who aid the dishonorable aid in dishonoring themselves.

Meekness

Meekness is not weakness; be firm, but also be compassionate; right is stronger than might.

The poor in spirit are rich in compassion.

Achievement

Where you work and how much you make do not make you what you are.

Commoners commonly believe they are common.

Useful men are useful to God.

Success means crossing the finish line.

Everyone has talent; if you identify your talents and use them, you will be successful.

Narrow visions narrow options.

Pleasure is not the only measure of success.

Your race cannot be won if it is run on someone else's track.

A ship sailing in the wrong sea cannot be righted.

Affirmation

The need for affirmation is an affirmation of weakness.

Quite often the most minimized are the most patronized.

Self-esteem runs out of steam.

Motivation will not last long if it is not long-lasting.

Self-exaltation

Vainglory is the main glory of pretentious men.

Those often touted by themselves often have nothing worth touting.

Braggers and daggers work better when they are sharp.

Deflated he goes who does not consider inflated egos.

He who exalts himself halts himself. [5]

The impressive do not impress God.

The least aggressive are most impressive. [38]

Strength and Weakness

All are mighty who are with the Almighty.

Those who choose God above all are all above.

Strength is self-evident in one's own self-evidence.

Strong people do not have to be reminded they are strong.

The only rival a strong man has is himself.

Better to be underestimated than to be overestimated.

Remaining weak takes strength.

It takes power not to use power.

The difference between the weak and the strong: weak men wrestle with God to gain approval for themselves, and strong men wrestle with themselves to gain approval from God.

Great men step in when everyone else steps out.

The measure of greatness is not if you can leave footprints, but whether or not those footprints remain after you are gone.

The difference between the great and the ordinary: great men provide great opportunities for others, and ordinary men provide ordinary opportunities for themselves.

When we try to be more than what we are, we become less than what we are, [39] and when we try to be less than what we are, we become more than what we are. [38]

When we realize we are nothing, that is when we become something. [40]

Knowing weakness is a known strength.

Ability

A man cannot do more than he can chew.

If man is your help, God help you.

Stagnation

Those who seek victory get victory.

The bold grow no mold.

You cannot possess new ground if old ground possesses you.

Holdings hold back.

Adversity

People never learn until they learn they are in danger.

A tumultuous storm caused a dying field to be flooded. Before the storm, the field was unproductive because it had not been cared for properly, and after the deluge, it was rejuvenated.

The field's workers felt as if their lives were over. They were immediately distraught and heartbroken following the aftermath. However, they quickly learned the flood washed away the infertile soil that had been plaguing them and brought in fresh rich earth. Their grief turned into joy as soon as they realized the field was not barren anymore, and they could grow crops abundantly once again.

This is the explanation of the parable: the storm represents difficulties, the field represents supports and livelihoods, and the fieldworkers represent individuals and populations.

Sometimes it takes a catastrophe to get us back on track. For if foolishness remains for too long, it is not long before nothing can be done. God has to rattle our cages from time to time, lest we become victims of our own poor stewardship. That which hurts has to be removed in order for the things that help to be brought in. Unfortunately, every so often adversity is the only thing which allows it to happen.

Every experience in failure is an experience to learn.

Great problems are great lessons.

Bad experiences can be good barricades.

Setbacks set drifters back on track.

Easy rides make for easy slides.

Painful lessons are best learned from others.

Perfectionism

Those who aim to be perfect always miss their target.

Compulsiveness

Compulsive behavior leads to repulsive behavior.

Self-control

Temptation and tribulation cannot be avoided.

You cannot control your thoughts, but you can control your actions.

Do not let the worst in you get the best of you.

Moral Standards

Before any moral judgments can be made, a strong moral foundation must be laid.

After the high bar is removed, every low bar becomes just as valid as any other.

Break down the dam of restraint, and a deluge of sin will ensue.

A wall once existed that kept invaders out of a city. This wall was originally constructed with sturdy bricks that would endure an attack. Over time, the sturdy bricks were replaced by weaker bricks so that the wall eventually collapsed. After the wall fell, invaders entered the city and looted its inhabitants.

This is the explanation of the parable: the wall represents morality, the city represents civilization, the sturdy bricks represent God's laws, the weaker bricks represent moral ambiguity, and the invaders represent sin.

Civilizations are always safer whenever they embrace God's laws, because God's commandments hold back sinners. Whenever moral ambiguity replaces divine law, morality changes, and morality that is not based upon absolutes, unlike absolute morality, is made up of weak tenets that collapse under their own weight.

Houses tumble after foundations crumble.

Anything baseless is faceless.

Moral arguments which are entirely material are entirely immaterial.

Matter does not matter.

Absolute morality is God's very nature; it is the standard by which all deeds are weighed, the rod that all actions are measured against.

Customs are customarily different, and *norms* normally are not the same; absolute morality, on the other hand, is recognized by everyone.

The difference between moral judgments and normal judgments: moral judgments apply to everyone, and normal judgments only apply to some.

Whether we want to admit it or not, we all live by moral standards—it just depends on whose standard we apply.

Morality cannot be legislated any more than reality can be mitigated.

Cafeteria Morality

Cafeteria morality is *idolatry*, and *situational ethics* does not situate ethically.

Commandments are not condiments; you cannot pick and choose the ones you like.

Atheism

Everybody believes in something; *atheists* and *agnostics* believe in nothing.

Atheism is the remedy of the guilty conscience, the god of a godless world—it is the narcotic of a morally destitute people.

Christianity is not a crutch; *atheism* is an excuse.

Atheists deny God because they do not deny themselves.

Those who think they are gods never think there is a God.

Humanists worship themselves because they do not worship God.

Internal Conflict

A man divided against himself cannot stand himself.

Those who know to hate themselves hate to know themselves.

Only a good man can take a good look at himself without feeling bad.

Mirrors bring terrors.

Men who avoid themselves, themselves avoid God.

He who runs to get away from himself always has his enemy at his tail.

Veils unveil truth.

Choices

Choices are chances.

Prudence

Good judgment makes a good ally, and prudence is a defense against decadence.

Depravity

Depravity is a cavity.

The most depraved men are the most enslaved men.

They are yielded who are not shielded.

Carelessness

What you do for cheers can enslave you for years, and what you do for approval might result in your immediate removal, for careless, hapless fun is a lot like playing with a dangerous, loaded gun.

A single night of carelessness could bring eighteen years of responsibility.

Some go under due to a blunder.

Idleness

Too much time and too little virtue fetches just enough wrath.

Idle hands trouble lands.

Addiction

Drugs nourish thugs.

Addiction leads to dereliction, and eventually it becomes one's darkest affliction.

To dull pain is not to annul pain.

Pain avoided can be voided.

Drugs amend sorrow rather than end sorrow.

Dope as a means to cope does not deliver hope.

Pot heads head nowhere, and crack heads are headed to crack.

Alcohol does two things: it fuels a fire, and it sinks a man deep in mire.

Bibbery makes slavery.

Drinkers and sinkers descend to the bottom.

Many a vices, many a crises

Sobriety is the key to stability.

Health

Miracles are not found in capsules.

Better to do naturally than chemically.

Medicine, like *jettison,* should be tossed out if it is not needed.

No insurance today keeps the doctor at bay.

Prevention is the best medicine for an ailing bottom line.

Well men stay well away from ill doctors who only seek pay.

Visit a doctor today if your health fades abruptly away.

Bereavement never ends when treatment is never-ending.

Perpetual infirmity perpetrates perpetual misery.

Big anxieties do more harm than slight fragilities.

People who always mind sickness always sicken their mind.

Unclean practices practice unclean health.

Dung enters the body just as easily as it exits it.

Decent exercise exercises decent health.

Doctors supply information, not salvation.

God's favor is better than any physician.

Comeliness is not seemly with ungodliness.

Feelings

Just because something feels right does not mean it is the right thing to do; sometimes the right feeling can give you the wrong expectation.

He is given over to his own appealings who is driven under by his own feelings.

Life and Death

Choose life, and you will not lose life. [41]

Those who fail to comprehend life avail to apprehend death.

To live, a man must die. [42]

CHAPTER 3

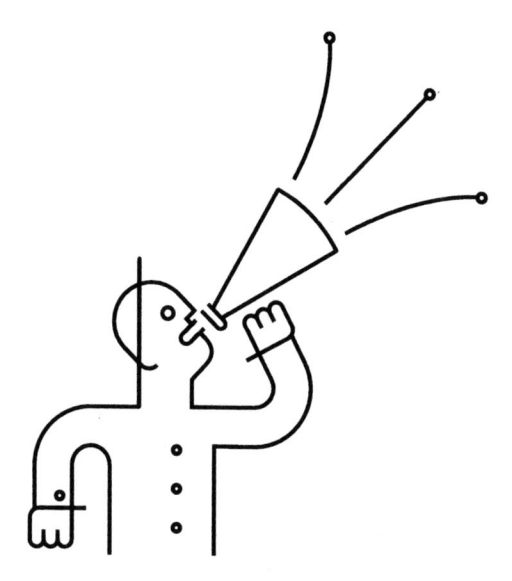

Relationships & Conflict

Inherent Strife

As the sun rises up each and every day, evil will be in man's each and every way.

The good fight [1] fights the bad plight.

Every soul is a soldier.

Occupants of the fallen world fall into a *Hot LZ*.

Birth births trouble.[2]

From womb to tomb there is unease, and in life there is always strife.

Those who strive for mastery master strife.[3]

Concord

To make a good team, we must be on the same team.

Spouses who belong to one another [4] get along with one another.

A mate is hard to hate.

Common ways pave the way for peace.

The likeminded never get blindsided.

Pledges are hedges against pandemonium, and covenants convey order.

Men and women live on the same planet when they dwell on the same principles.

Different genders were not engendered differently.[5]

Empathy is the path to harmony.

Doing right instead of wrong is the key to getting along.

Discord

Poor harmonies spoil rich symphonies.

People who never agree always agree to part.

Groups at odds cannot be in league.

Friction is a function of opposing forces.

Discord dislodges peace.

Contentment does not live with resentment.

Ethnic Fighting

Black and white fight when they always think they are right.

Cultural gaps spark racial scraps.

Cultural differentiation is more caustic than genetic variation.

Different genes, different nationalities, different cultures, different nations

Equality

Common threads lead to a common source.

There are no good guys, only none that do good. [6]

Everyone is just as less than God as everyone else.

A diamond amid coal is still carbon.

When everyone is treated with equal respect and with equal contempt, only then will there be equality.

Peacetakers

There is no serenity for the workers of iniquity. [7]

Scorn is the horn which pierces amity, and wrath is the bath which stews enmity.

Debauched men botch everything.

Those who always want to best everyone never rest with anyone.

Peacemakers

Peacemakers and saltshakers dispense enrichment.

Grudge

A sin that is not forgotten is never forgiven.

It is hard to grasp the future if you are clutching the past.

A grudge will keep you deep in sludge.

Points of contention are points of retention.

Holdups uphold dissent.

Spite

The froward never go forward, and the hostile never reconcile.

The rancorous become cantankerous.

Spite and light linger until switched off.

Revenge

Revenge is hard to reverse.

Assistance does more good than resistance. [8]

Reconciliation

Newness heads in after oldness heads out.

If you want to get right with yourself and others, first get right with God.

Peace with God, peace with all

Consideration

One man's freedom is another man's oppression.

The right of one person is the *blight* of another.

Consider your neighbor, and he will consider you.

Mercy is reciprocated unto the merciful.[9]

Consider God and others, and you will not sin against either of them.

Thoughtfulness is the mark of righteousness.

Self-centeredness

Do not push others down to pull yourself up, and never make someone look bad so you can look good.

He who puts himself first puts everyone else last.

Those who serve themselves, themselves are the servants of pride.

To love oneself above all is to hate all selflessness.

Deterrence

Run away when you see a godless man coming toward you, or else you may see yourself going with him toward perdition.

Better to turn away than to burn away.[10]

Separate from sin before it separates you from God.

Trust

Never put faith in people who have no faith.

Trust people who trust in God.

Everyone is worthy of suspicion when no one is worthy of trust.

Surely *surety* is the only way to trust a fool.

Honor

Severed honor severs all hope.

Better to die in honor than to live in shame.

Self-condemnation

Self-condemnation is the first step toward self-preservation.

Judgment is sacrificed through self-sacrifice. [11]

Before you can rely on yourself, you must deny yourself.

Those who deny themselves are not denied. [12]

Justice

Judge righteously, not self-righteously.

Justice is never attained through injustice.

Erected injustice is not corrected justice.

Never oppress the innocent to punish the guilty, and do not destroy one life to save another.

Punishing the innocent for transgressions their ancestors committed is not an end to discrimination but an amend to discrimination.

Exploit

Exploiting big mistakes is the biggest mistake.

Exploiters exploit the exploited.

Thugs and bugs profit from decay.

Oppression

Down the road the downtrodden tread upon the heavily laden.

Masses oppress once they are oppressed.

Today's alienated become tomorrow's alienators.

Victims quickly turn into victimizers.

If strangers outnumber estrangers, the estrangers become endangered.

First, the oppressed are taken advantage of; then they take advantage of everyone else.

Children of oppressors become victims of oppressed children.

First, parents kill children in abortion clinics, and then children kill parents in *euthanasia* centers.

Disparity

Much poverty precedes much *tyranny*.

The poor take it all once the rich make it all.

Epidemic flaps worsen whenever economic gaps widen.

Longevity

Nobody wants to live forever when everybody wants to live forever.

Longing to live forever does not guarantee a long life.

Lack of Restraint

Everything goes when anything goes.

Nothing is possible when everything is possible.

The more willing we are to do anything, the less likely it is that anything good will happen.

A rancher with a rodent problem thought to himself, *vipers eat rats, they might help*. One day the rancher gathered some vipers together, and he let them go in his field. The next morning he learned his plan failed; he still had a rodent problem, but now things were worse—the vipers had poisoned his livestock.

This is the explanation of the parable: the rancher represents misguided problem solvers, the rats represent problems, and the vipers represent immoral solutions.

Immoral solutions are worse than any problem we could face; they have unintended consequences, and more often than not, they do not alleviate the problems they are set out to solve. They just add newer, more severe problems to a preexisting list of old problems.

Good intentions have bad results.

Man's right wrongs him. [13]

Infection

Your sin is not just your problem.

One stumbles because another fumbles.

Reaches of sin go far beyond the sinner; the sins of the fathers go farther. [14]

Wounded souls wound everyone.

Child Rearing

Broken adults beget broken children, and foul parents foul their offspring.

Strange children come from strangers to God. [15]

Loose parents loosen evil. [16]

It does not take a village to raise a child, it takes good parents; good parents make good citizens, and good citizens make good civilizations.

Edification foils indoctrination.

The instructed become instructors.

To not chasten a child is to hasten his death. [17]

Judged children are not delivered before judges, and exhorted children do not become incarcerated adults.

Parental neglect prompts government parenting.

The unsustained look for sustenance wherever they can find it.

Children who are not told what is up and what is down, what is right and what is wrong, usually end up singing a very sad song.

Children wail when parents fail, and honor is not parented when parents are not honored.

Humans bemoan when their children are alone. [16]

Often, failures were failed.

Tell a child what to do, and he will do it only when you tell him; show him by example, and he will do it always. [18]

The chained cannot go anywhere, and the happy do not go anywhere.

Deterioration

Where no one fears God, everyone fears man.

When the good are few, few are the good times.

Happiness is in low supply when godliness is in low regard.

You cannot win if you dwell in sin. [19]

Victory is elusive wherever godly ways are preclusive.

Good expectations are not expected whenever bad inclinations are not rejected.

Bad Company

Note the person who quickly learns an evil man's ways: he learns quickly he is on his way to ruin.

Stupid friends go before stupid decisions.

Friends of fools are befriended by foolishness.

Foolish fellows love fellowship.

Lame brains and *lampreys* attach themselves to swifter beings.

Better to dwell alone than to dwell amongst fools.

Hell is expelled along with *hellions*. [20]

Difficulty and Complexity

Complex problems are the result of the actions of simple people.

The world looks complicated when the mind gets constipated.

War

Where there are no instigators, there are no wars.

Malice is the chalice that serves up war. [21]

Wars are great when hearts do hate.

God does not have to destroy the world; if human beings are left to their own devices, they will destroy it for Him.

Better to end a war than to start one.

Firearms

Unmanned arms are safer than unarmed men.

Men kill without guns, but guns do not kill without men.

Taking a Stand

If thou durst stand thy ground, thou wilt not be ground to dust.

Draw a line in the dirt, or else you will be buried in it.

You can either come to the fight, or the fight will come to you.

The man who gives an inch takes a chance.

Firm stances curb vague chances.

Stood ground is good ground.

Pacifism

Those who never shove back always get shoved in the back.

Pacifism never prevents war; at best, it only postpones it.

There are times when no one dies because something is done, and there are other times when everyone dies because nothing is done.

Rules of Engagement

Only go to war if the result of not fighting is worse than the result of fighting.

Violence is viable in situations friable.

The first rule to any engagement: put God first.

Never start a war; always end them.

Always drop the option of peace before dropping the bomb.

Warn to go away before you blow away.

Methodology and Tactics

The right battle is lost with the wrong weapon.

Do not artillery shell a shell artillery, or team swat a SWAT team.

Those who work smart do not have to work as hard.

Remember the A-B-C rule: ALWAYS BE CAREFUL!

A-C-E it: first **assess**, then **collect**, and finally **execute**. [22]

Do one thing: do God's will.

It is well to do the will of God.

Methodology matters.

How the fight is done can determine if the fight is won.

Before you attack the line, establish a line of attack. [22]

Set up a *beachhead* before you reach ahead.

Let everything fall into place before you place your first shot. [22]

Intelligent actions come by way of actionable *intelligence*.

Good *logistics* prevent bad statistics.

Peaceful Existences

The possibility of war enhances the probability of peace.

The fear of war makes peace.

Content populations are peaceful populations, and they are populations that will not rise up.

Believers and nonbelievers can coexist as long as they are not forced to drink from the same ideological cup.

From the *Sword* comes peace. [23]

Division

Wherever ideologies collide, there is a great divide.

A house divided never balks to *Balkanize*. [24]

The divided are easily derided.

Volatility

All gets obliterated when pressures are not mitigated.

Because he thought it would suit him, a foolish scientist stored volatile chemicals together without considering the consequence. This stupid scientist was unaware of the precarious situation he placed himself and his colleagues under. One day the chemicals leaked out, and they came in contact with each other, resulting in a huge blast.

This is the explanation of the parable: the scientist represents *demagogues*, the chemicals represent immiscible ideologies or cultures, and the laboratory and the scientist's colleagues represent peoples and nations.

Clashes are unavoidable wherever conflicting cultures meet. If people feel threatened, it is only natural at some point that they will fight. *Demagogues* throw incompatible groups together because it suits them politically, and whenever there are quarrels, instead of uniting people together, they exploit the situation further for even more political gain, until one day the powder keg explodes, and there is mayhem and civil war.

The proud are loud when they have a shroud, but as soon as their actions bring riot, they fast become quiet.

Freedom of Conscience

Without freedom of conscience, freedom is not conscious.

True self-determination determines true freedom.

Individual liberty liberates individuals.

Detested behaviors ought never to become behested behaviors.

Torn consciences tear nations apart.

Incompatibility

Any time fifty percent of the population goes one direction, and fifty percent in the other, one hundred percent of the populace is in serious risk of experiencing a major upheaval.

The plow gets broke whenever divided oxen are placed under one single *yoke*.

A naïve welder tried fusing diverse metals together without using a flux. Because the welder did not use flux, he ended up with an incompletely fused product that eventually fell apart.

This is the explanation of the parable: the naïve welder represents diversity without unity, the metals represent ethnic and religious groups, and the flux represents commonalities.

Diverse groups *Balkanize* whenever there is nothing holding them together. If people are to come together and stay together, shared commonalities need to be stressed rather than social discords.

Refuge

There has to be a refuge from refuse.

Brutes

Basic men basically understand force.

Thugs only understand thuggery.

It is simple: simple people are simply beasts. [25]

Turmoil

Tyranny quells warring factions when all else fails, and what *despots* do to maintain peace is more frightening than war itself.

Bedlam puts freedom to bed.

Crises and *feces* breed parasites.

Unity

Too often, unity remains in brevity.

Egalitarianism

Civilizations never reach *equilibrium* because they are never equal.

Inequality remains with *egalitarianism* just as *botulism* still exists with starvation.

Leveling one playing field bevels another.

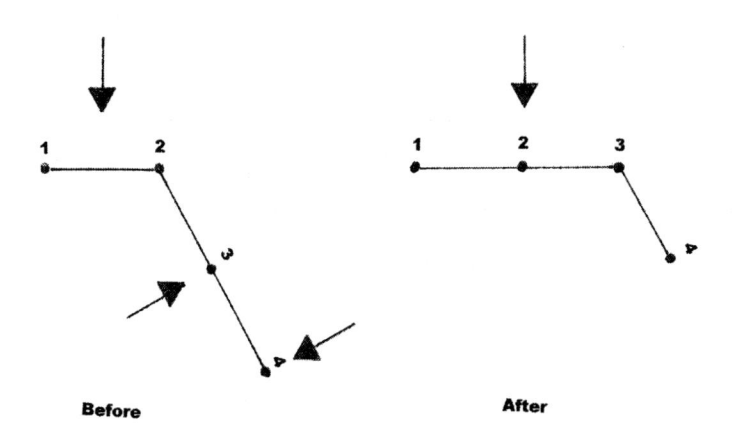

Before   **After**

Political and Financial Instability

First there is *anarchy*, then calamity, then calamity is intolerable, and it gives way to *tyranny*, then *tyranny* is oppressive, and the pendulum swings back to *anarchy*.

Capitalism takes courage, and *communism* takes freedom away; this is why pure *capitalism* and *communism* are rarely seen.

Aggravation and Insecurity

People take until they can take no more taking.

They burn who have nowhere to turn.

If you give a man room, you might see him run; if you back him into a corner, you could see a gun.

A lion struck in the back strikes back.

Tensions make dissensions.

Wherever there is frustration, there is sedition.

Insecurity secures instability.

Survival of the Weakest

The man tied to a slave becomes a slave.

They cannot live fully who are fully held back.

There is less help when all are helpless.

Strong men do not always lift weak men, but weak men always bring down strong men.

The lowest common denominator dominates.

Tolerance

Tolerating all together is altogether intolerable.

You cannot force someone to be tolerant without being intolerant toward their intolerance.

Offense

The man offended by all is upended by all.

When defenses are strong, offenses are weak.

Offending the truth for the sake of the offended is most offensive.

Modern Multiculturalism

Anything strict is strictly doctrinal.

Modern *multiculturalism* is *monoculturalism*.

Inclusiveness

Inclusiveness includes including evil and excluding absolutes.

Permissiveness

Just fitting in fits in with just giving in.

Permissive behavior is submissive behavior.

To tolerate sin is to advocate death.

A housewife made dinner for her family every night. Her family's favorite foods were toxic, and she knew it. Despite her own concerns, she kept feeding her family the deadly fodder night after night because she did not want to offend them. One evening her family demanded and ate an extra portion, and they all died.

This is the explanation of the parable: the housewife represents watchmen, [26] the family represents loved ones who embrace sin, and the toxic foods represent immoral behavior.

You cannot tolerate immoral behavior, even if it is out of love, without being complicit. If you keep turning a blind eye every time the people you love sin, their blood will be on your hands. [27]

Being nice does not always suffice.

The cruelest thing to do is to permit cruelty.

Indifference is no different than insurgence.

Admonition

Tough stances turn away weak standards.

Admonishment prevents astonishment.

Better to rebuke than to remorse.

Yell on the rooftop before hell blows the roof off.

The *shofar* has been a great weapon so far.

Intercession

Prayer is a slayer. [28]

To not pray is to become prey.

Stubbornness

They are always in mourning who never heed warning.

Stiff-necked men are aloof to reproof. [29]

Pack Mentality

Crowds are shrouds for bad behavior.

Men pleasers and business ventures need approval.

He who fits in fits out. [30]

To cleave, you must leave. [31]

Worldly Persecution

The strong in the world are weak in God, [32] and the strong in God are weak in the world. [33]

It is not so much that sinners hate righteousness as much as they love wickedness so much.

The world cannot stand those who stand for Christ. [34]

God's selected are rejected. [34]

Often, the most wronged are the most right.

Men most hated by the most hated men are most beloved.

People aligned with good are maligned by evil.

Better to hear worldly derision than to bear godly indignation.

The persecuted are preferred. [35]

Violent Resistance

Fighters in rings could be kings, and fighters in bars could be behind them.

Surely you will be met with violence if you resist with violence. [36]

Resist, but resist righteously.

Before serpents can be defeated, they must be defanged.

A large anaconda had a man in its coils. The man struggled with the enormous snake and resisted violently. The more intensely the man fought, the more the anaconda constricted. Eventually, the man died as a result of the enormous pressure he was forced to endure.

This is the explanation of the parable: the large anaconda represents tyrannical government, and the man represents oppressed citizenries.

It is only natural for people to lash out whenever they feel threatened, but when you are dealing with a shrewd enemy, you must be shrewd. Tyrants want us to resist them so they can clamp down on us. Do not play their game; resist them, but do it as peaceably as you can. Fire off ballots instead of bullets, and drop in with your neighbor and have a discussion, but never drop bombs in any buildings.

Monsters make martyrs.

Swords do not convert souls.

Messages do more good than massacres.

Better to exchange ideas than to exchange blows.

The difference between sedition and revolution: the number involved in the evolution.

A lone rebel revolting is revolting.

There is little success when little is involved.

Haste

Occasionally, the game is won when nothing is done.

The first to the slaughter is the first to be slaughtered.

The race to nowhere does not avail because it does not prevail.

Often, the greatest men are the latest men.

A farmer planted seeds one spring, hoping they would bear fruit by summer. When mid spring rolled around, the farmer's seeds had not yet germinated, and by early summer, the result was the same. The farmer left his field at the end of that period dejected because he thought his effort had failed.

The following spring, the farmer saw lush plants in his field in great number. The previous year's seeds were lying dormant, and by the time the farmer decided to sow another crop, he already had what he needed to feed himself and his family for the rest of the season.

This is the explanation of the parable: the farmer represents *Christians*, the seeds represent godly endeavors, and the lush plants represent blessings from God.

You never know exactly when God will bless your labors.[37] Never feel dismal if you are doing God's will; just keep sowing seed. Ultimately, God will provide everything you need to glorify Him, and you will be blessed as a byproduct. First seek God, and everything will be added to you.[38]

Be ready for everything, but be prepared to do nothing.

Those who press the situation get pressed by the situation.

Strike when targets present, and never relent.

Better to make the last move than to make the first one.

Inactivity is not always the product of inability.

All goes awry whenever R&D is done on the fly.

Foresight

Think ahead before you make your first move, or you might be dead before you make your last one.

Mates who fail to check never fail to get checkmated.

Foreseen conflicts can be averted before they see the light of day.

Smart men run from danger; wise men avoid it altogether.

Better to prevent than to lament.

Overload

Do not be a dunce by taking on too much at once.

Many tight aims produce many loose ends.

Multitude of tasks, multitude of mishaps

Full plates are full of turmoil.

Waste makes haste.

Unfinished jobs finish slobs.

Excessive undertakings take under excessively.

To agree to more is to see to less.

He who minds much binds little.

Full hands never clinch fully.

Your life becomes a job whenever a job becomes your life.

Inability

No system leads to systematic failure.

He is found lacking who lacks to find backing.

No might, no fight

Those with no shoulders cannot shoulder burden.

Except you have what it takes, you cannot take what is yours.

Unless a man can see the bridge, he cannot bridge the sea. [39]

It is easier to picture big if you see the big picture.

Sameness

The same road has the same potholes.

Indicators

Bad indicators are good indicators that adjustments have to be made.

Advancement

The last to begin are the first to end.

Keep on growing as you keep on going.

Mobile forces are able forces.

Attraction and Infatuation

Do not be concerned if you are attracted to the opposite sex; be concerned if you are not. If you like the opposite sex, that just means you are in working order.

The difference between attraction and obsession: attraction is a natural affinity, and obsession is an unnatural proclivity.

Infatuations and medications wear off; likewise, passions and fashions go out of style.

Lust

Lust and rust break down integrity.

The difference between someone who loves and someone who lusts: lovers consider their mate, and lusters consider themselves.

Objectification

Let beauty be appreciated, but never allow it to be depreciated.

Objectification of the body leads to desecration of the mind.

The Male/Female Relationship

Male and female are different halves of the same whole.[40]

When two lovers give, they each receive.

It takes more than one stick to spark a flame.

Desires and fires need fuel.

Loveless sex is listless sex, and commoditized sex is lobotomized sex.

Promiscuity dilutes potency, and saturation hinders maturation.

Heat is never felt where cold is never dealt.

Sweet and sour gives flavor much more power.

Women are the gatekeepers of virtue; lost women make lost civilizations.

Discrete women are *mete* women.

Girls and boys are not toys.

Men and women lose contact with each other when they become loose with each other.

Anything easy to get gets easy to let.

Women lose power when they lose influence.

Harlotry

Those that *know* often are often known.

It is hard to recover from an easy reputation.

Whores and boars get soiled.

Harlots and rodents attract snakes.

The Sexual Revolution

The *Sexual Revolution* revolutionized man's evolution toward despair.

Sexual freedom brings carnal slavery.

Destruction of the Family

To redefine civil marriage is to redefine civilization.

Destroy the family, and you will become familiar with destruction.

CHAPTER 4

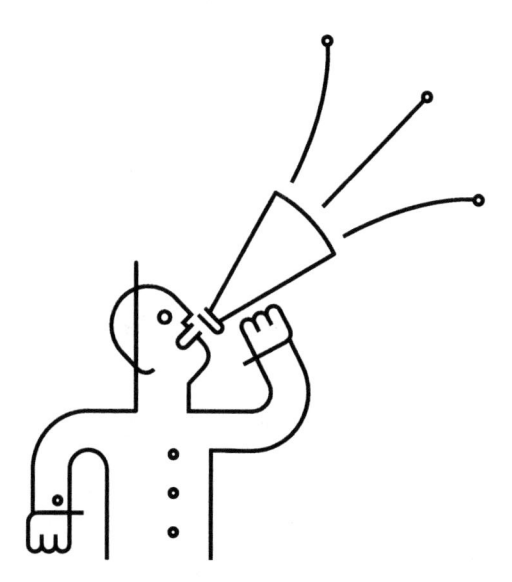

Hearts & Minds

Noise

Shrill noises drown out still voices.

It is hard to be heard amongst a herd.

Overwhelming Concern

Those with no time to spare have no time to care.

Time is one of the most valuable gifts a person can give.

Big concerns leave little room for concern.

When cares are begotten, God is forgotten.

Wisdom

Wisdom from above comes out of love,[1] and wisdom from within comes out of sin.[2]

Wisdom is more akin to vision than intelligence.[3]

Intelligent men think, and wise men watch.

Wise men are fed instead of taught.

A speck of wisdom plants forests,[4] and a heap of folly brings them down.[5]

Wisdom becomes foolishness when foolishness becomes wisdom.

Strength fails, but wisdom avails.

Experience

Only those experienced in wisdom are made wise by experience.

The longest ages do not always make for the strongest *sages*.[6]

Sight

An open eye is better than an open mind.

Where there is no vision, there is no way.

What we understand is limited by what we see; to know more, we must see more.

Questions and Answers

New answers from old liars need to be questioned.

Endless questions beg for useless answers.

Anything fathomable is answerable.

Hard questions abound wherever easy answers astound.

Hard questions require soft answers.

Dull answers from sharp intellects are like poisons prescribed from doctors.

Obstinacy

Closed mouths do not receive food, and obstinate hearts cannot conceive knowledge.

Pestilence kills the body, and obstinacy the mind.

Those who never change their spots are always easy to spot.

Discernment

A discerning mind is better than a learning mind.

Cheap Rhetoric

The best fools give the worst advice.

Do not heed wisdom from the mouths of boobs, and never be fooled by charismatics who lack character.

Reject intellectuals without intellect.

Sound bites sound real good—that is, until reality takes a good sound bite out of your arse.

Serpent tongues snake everywhere but head nowhere.

Pointless attitudes make for endless *platitudes*.

Understanding

The man who does not understand arithmetic cannot be taught calculus.

One's own understanding is one's own downfall. [7]

Maturity

Learn in youth, and you will not be an old learner.

Foolishness always remains when youth never ends.

Those full of maturity are full of possibility.

The Exchange of Ideas

Pupils attending most institutions of higher learning are encouraged to explore every possibility, except the possibility that Jesus Christ is the Son of God and the Savior of the world.

Religion and politics are the only subjects worth discussing.

Discourse

Discourse is not necessarily discord.

A good debate is bad to negate.

The Rise of Iniquity

Wickedness is raised when goodness is sunk.

The bad are lifted when the good are shifted.

Hostility Toward God

Those who attempt *deicide* commit suicide.[8]

To provoke God is to invoke judgment.

Those who strive with God strive for death.

The man who fights with his Maker fights to make himself a marker.[9]

Control

Big fools are great tools, and old hippies deceive young druggies.

To crave very much is to become very much a slave.

Wanted desires require *tribute*.

People controlled by their lusts are easy to control, and weak believers are easily swayed by strong deceivers.

Degenerates and marionettes are restricted by cords.

They are readily played whose minds are easily swayed.

Indulgence

Weak spirits are fed by strong indulgences; people who love excess hate restraint.

Folks who only seek elation always neglect to receive salvation.

Blindness

If blindness is your guide, darkness is your destination.

Awareness

Convincing a knowledgeable lamb is harder than controlling an ignorant lion.

Alert populaces are greater forces than ones left in the dark.

Asking a question is easier than hearing an answer, and answers hurt when answers reveal.

Knowledge is dreaded when virtue is shredded.

That which is enlightening can be frightening.

Abhorrent reality is a threat to apparent security.

With many thoughts come many fraughts. [10]

Lack of Knowledge

Blissful ignorance is full of peril.

Men void of understanding avoid understanding.

Those who have no knowledge have no chance.

Men become history when they fail to learn it.

Lack of Concern

The beguiled never get riled, and the least engaged are the least enraged.

Those who have no care for thought have their thoughts cared for.

If you never care to know, you will never know to care.

People always die when they never ask why.

Little concern delivers little result.

You cannot fend for yourself if you cannot think for yourself.

Christianity and Christians

To make concrete, you need cement and water, and to be a concrete *Christian*, you need faith and truth.

A group was given a jewel to hold. One man decided to let the jewel tarnish, another dirtied it, and one even tried to sell it. The jewel was in such bad shape as time went on that its true value was not even known. One day a man visiting the group looked at the jewel and said, "This jewel is quite unique. There is not another like it; the jewel's value is far beyond the price of anything." The group stood there dumbfound because they had not realized what they had in their possession.

This is the explanation of the parable: the jewel represents *Christianity*, and the group represents *Christians*. The man who let the jewel tarnish represents *Christians* who neglect their faith, the man who dirtied it represents *Christians* who pollute the *Gospel* with false doctrines, and the man who tried to sell it represents *Christians* who sell out to *Satan*.

Christians squander opportunities every time they let their own personal fallacies get in the way of God's mission. Instead of bringing light to the world, many *Christians* have brought confusion. Christ is a gift, *Christians* are allowing God's gift to become another article of trade, and consequently, *Christianity* has not been brought to its fullest potential.

Apostasy

Before there is *apostasy*, there is *idolatry*.

Danger lurches from renegade churches.

Many houses of worship do not house worshippers. [11]

False prophets profess falsehoods, and what a true prophet says truly comes to pass. [12]

There is nothing more loathing than wolves in sheep's clothing.

Rebellious teachers teach rebellious preachers.

Ignorant ministers administer ignorance.

Pastors are disasters who lead to wayward pastures.

Apostates and phosphates act as fertilizers.

If the devil takes over, take a hike.

Give the boot to *bootlickers*, and kick them to the curb who curb the *Word of God*.

The Bible

Read the *Word of God* to seed the WORD OF GOD.

A *Christian* without a Bible is like a knight without a sword.

Preparedness

Those who go in blind come out behind.

Preparing for victory prepares victory.

Details

Details detail validity, and definitions define legitimacy.

A **bull** grazing in a fair plain is not the same as a **bull** bucking on an airplane.

Whether or not a word can be maligned mostly depends on how that word is defined.

Collateral Damage

Always hit your mark, for every missed bullet is a missed opportunity.

Collateral damage damages any case already made.

An acclaimed chef placed a phony ingredient inside a popular dish. Before he added the item, his patrons could not have been more pleased, and after he introduced it, they could not have been more disgusted. All the work he did to build his restaurant went by the wayside because he allowed one simple mistake.

This is the explanation of the parable: the acclaimed chef represents reputable arguments, the phony ingredient represents shoddy information, and the chef's patrons represent the listening public.

Shoddy information brings down reputable arguments all the time. It is not uncommon for entire cases to fold simply because someone did not do the proper inspection. Good points need to be supported by good facts. If one claim an arguer makes is untrustworthy, all his claims are untrustworthy.

Words

That which proceeds from the mouth first proceeds from the heart.[13]

Evil throats produce evil notes.

Good words from bad mouths and bad words from good mouths shock every ear they enter.

Men who never say always, and who always say never, rarely say anything deemed to be clever.

Vetting

Those who always vet what the say never regret what they say.

Multitude of Words

Detritus nourishes detractors.

Easy speech and *speakeasies* are open to prosecution.

Loose tempers lose arguments.

He who squeals too much reveals too much.

Few Words

To avoid retort, keep your answers simple and short.

Fewer words, fewer *gaffes*

Straight shots avert late shots.

Kept tongues keep their keepers.

To conceal knowledge is to congeal knowledge. [14]

Character Assassins

Personnel attackers resort to personal attacks.

That which cannot be offed by the world gets scoffed by the world.

A wicked guide took some unsuspecting people down a perilous road. He discredited his competitor before he got underway and claimed his journey way would be safe for everyone involved.

Just as the trek got started, the road began to claim its first victims; it did not take long for the people to find themselves in harm's way. One by one they fell, and the wicked guide was powerless to help. While the people were perishing, the wicked guide's competitor rushed down to assist them, but they would not accept his aid because the wicked guide vilified him. All the unsuspecting people and their guide died on the road that day with support standing right next to them.

This is the explanation of the parable: the wicked guide represents *humanists*, the wicked guide's competitor represents *Christians*, and the perilous road represents life.

It is getting harder and harder for *Christians* to help people these days because *humanists* keep vilifying them. Western culture is saturated with anti-Christian and pro-humanist images in the media. *Christians* almost always look bad in popular entertainment and in academia, so it is no wonder they are becoming a *pariah*. The sad part is that *humanism* is not going to save anyone from the dangers we face; only God can do that. If people continue to be turned off to the message of the *gospel*, there are going to be far more casualties on the road of life.

Bad accusations destroy good reputations.

Those who hate speaking to accusers accuse others of hate speech.

Big *bigots* bawl *bigotry*.

Malcontents are malicious, and the *noisome* are noisy.

The noisiest complainers are the lousiest restrainers.

Light and Darkness

Light penetrates darkness, but darkness does not penetrate light.

There can be no darkness where there is light.

Truth

You cannot battle truth.

That which is right is difficult to fight.

Truth stands firm under firm assault.

Truth is avoided because it cannot be voided.

Death lies where truth dies.

Lies and Liars

Lies cannot change the world; they only change the way it is perceived.

Liars always have an advantage because they never have to be right.

Liars desire more *hire*.

The only thing more dangerous than a lie is a lie mixed with truth.

Lies go hidden wherever truth is not bidden.

They lie in danger who listens to lies.

Big lies and small flies spread disease.

Fraud and Charlatans

The puffed up blow up when they cannot put up.

Frauds flee when they can no longer fake.

The snide deride as a means to hide, and the vain feign to avoid pain.

The confounded get dumbfounded.

Thieves and sheaths hide devices.

A crook will *rook*.

Slavery begins with *knavery*.

Relativism and Existentialism

There is nothing more untrue than everything is true.

The absolute statement "THERE ARE NO ABSOLUTES" is absolutely wrong.

People who do not acknowledge real truth acknowledge themselves real fools.

Moral *existentialism* exists in a moral vacuum.

One night a pernicious man replaced signs along a freeway with signs that had no meaning. The next day a woman drove down the same road where the signs had been replaced earlier, and she slammed into a car full of people, killing everyone involved.

This is the explanation of the parable: the pernicious man represents *existentialists*, the signs represent misinformation, and the woman and people in the car represent the innocent.

Innocent people are being harmed because *existentialists* are confusing the masses. All they care about is redefining truth so they can do whatever they want. Sadly, however, unsuspecting individuals are the casualties whenever *existentialists* attempt to replace truthful words with nebulous rhetoric.

Relativists believe in *relativism* until they or their loved ones are victims.

Relativism is a means to an end; it means to end all truth.

Relativists cannot stand truth because it stands in their way.

Rogues and worms hate light.

Something relative is relative to something.

There is no substitute for substance.

Utilitarianism

Sooner or later, *utilitarianism* loses its utility.

Secularism

A naive farmer diverted an old stream in order to irrigate a new field. Before the farmer redirected the flow of water, the stream was lively and ran unimpeded from its source, and after he rerouted the current, the stream dried up because it was cut off from its original spring.

This is the explanation of the parable: the naive farmer represents *secularists*, the new field represents secular societies, the old stream represents blessings from God, and the stream's original spring represents God Himself.

Secularists believe even if they shift resources in a new direction away from God toward evil, they can still receive the same blessings they had before. The truth is when men forsake God, He forsakes them. [15] *Secularists* also believe it is possible for them to use the Lord's old blessings to feed their new secular ideology. Again, that is folly and error. You cannot drink the cup of the Lord and the cup of devils in unison. [16]

For when truth is starved, there is starvation for truth.

Manure is a great fertilizer.

Out of *secularism* comes a yearning for God.

Humanism

Humanism is a crime against humanity.

Futility

It is a crime to mime the sublime.

Any nation whose foundation is imagination is on the road to decimation.

Freedom from reality ends up being enslavement to futility.

Vainful thoughts eventually give rise to painful thoughts.

Fools

Fools only fool other fools.

Fools follow feelings instead of facts.

The difference between a dummy and a fool: dummies hit the break when they are about to go over a cliff, but fools hit the accelerator.

Robots

Automatons automatically announce antiquated arguments, and reprobates regurgitate ridiculous refuse.

The opinions of minions are not their own.

Spiteful Mouths

The demonic demonize because they cannot demonstrate.

Backbiters and pit vipers spew venom.

Slanderers and salamanders dwell in muck.

Loose Tongues

Gossipers and grasshoppers jump in any chance they get.

Meddlers and peddlers interfere and annoy.

Avoid rattlers and babblers. [17]

Flattery

Flatteries and batteries spark dangerous energies. [18]

Conditioning

A conditioned mind is a terrible thing to waste your time hearing.

Conformed mind, deformed spirit

Enslaved minds do not mind slavery.

Minds consoled by evil are controlled by evil.

Implanted ideas produce supplanted ideals.

Before good men follow, bad men *fallow*.

Propaganda

Monolithic inking generates *monolithic* thinking.

Social engineering engineers *socialism*.

Deployers of *PSYOPS* and Cyclops see the world through one eye.

Readers of propagandist *blogs* are like *Ivan Pavlov's dogs*.

Lap dogs lap up propaganda.

Political Correctness

If you speak *political correctness*, you speak newspeak. [19]

Political correctness is the primary vehicle by which viewpoints not in line with an established way of thinking are eliminated.

Volition

Volition ought not to determine position.

Faulty Information

Those that fake history make history.

Faulty notions are the fault of haughty potions.

Fiction causes friction.

Loose facts lose souls.

Disbelief

Disbelief displaces faith.

Much doubt, little route

Arguments

Anything self-refuting is self-defeating.

Arguments which are not absolute absolutely crumble.

An argument without reason marks insanity is in season.

Arguing with idiots is arguably idiotic. [20]

Speaking to fools speaks to one's own foolishness.

Education

When education becomes indoctrination, the schooled get fooled.

Hijacked schools turn out instructed tools.

Often, the well educated are well subjugated.

Students of conceit study deceit.

Schooling educates, but knowledge liberates. [21]

Know-It-Alls

The most learned learn the least.

A know-it-all can throw it all if he never stops to think that he can blow it all.

They know not anything who think they know everything. [22]

Elitism

Academics and *ungulates* belch gas.

Elites and petites overestimate their weight.

Leniency

Deficiency is hard to see in a sea of leniency.

Rotten apples do not smell amid rotting apples.

One-sidedness

Vinegar is not bitter to those who have not tasted honey.

If all you know is evil, and you have never known good, you will never know good is better than evil.

Evil always looks better whenever goodness is trapped inside a *fetter*.

Unchallenged ideas challenge new ones.

Questions cannot be answered if answers cannot be questioned.

Desensitization

When sin becomes comfortable, it becomes deadly.

Sin feels good until you stop feeling.

Desensitization leads to annihilation.

Diversion

People used to distraction should get used to destruction.

Diversions divert attentions away from subversions.

All play and no work makes Jack a dullard boy.

Stimulation

Natural men naturally respond to stimulus.

Unstimulated minds mind no stimulation.

The confused are easily amused.

Amusement

Few clowns make for many chuckles, though too much stupidity brings very little hilarity.

Wherever folly releases, laughter ceases.

Social Decay

Fame for shame is evidence of civilizations gone lame.

It is only after society is rotten that people begin to smell the stench of reality.

Societal decay is the path to *sociopathic* behavior.

It does not take a prude to know the world is lewd.

Impulsiveness and Recklessness

Impulsiveness leads to destructiveness.

Reckless nations become feckless nations.

Fast lives make for quick deaths.

Those who live in the moment live momentarily.

In the realm of the here and now lie the there and gone.

Dangerous proclivities stem from heightened *brain stem* activities.

Those routinely *laid* by many people are routinely laid to rest by many transgressions.

The carnage of *carnality* is a stark reality.

Hedonism

With evil enjoyments come bitter attachments.

Corrupted Cultures

Junk foods and junk cultures have much in common; they are easy to obtain, and they have very little value associated with them.

Corrupt cultures corrupt everything, and corrupt values are valueless.

Insipidness

Those who sip emptiness drink up insipidness.

The Mind

Genes build the body, and *ethos* the mind.

Psychology and morphology shape everything.

The mind is for thinking, and the heart is for sinking.

A stopped mind cannot stop itself.

Minds that never think never think they will mind.

Good Sense

Good sense makes a good base.

Simply natural, naturally simple

Common Sense

Common sense is uncommon among the commonly corrupted.

Conventional wisdom becomes unconventional if conventions change.

Soundness

Sound wisdom sounds odd in a world deaf to God.

Abandoned Logic

To abandon reason is to embrace treason.

A world without logic is toxic.

Foolishness in Charge

Idiotic *idioms* make everyone idiots.

Nitwits are notable when nobles are numbskulls.

Pearls get hurled when *churls* get *Earled*.

When fools are cool, the feeble are able. [23]

Entertainment

It is hard to say whether the entertainment industry corrupted society, or society corrupted the entertainment industry. Supply stems from demand; if the public rejected filth, the entertainment industry would not produce it. Entertainment is a business; if entertainers were to produce items the public would not buy, they would not be in business for very long. There is plenty of blame for the entertainment industry, but some blame has to rest on consumers as well. If viewers and listeners do not want to see or hear rubbish on their airwaves, they should not purchase it.

Bad entertainment entertains bad behavior.

Convolution

They are mixed who mix right and wrong.

When you make evil good, and good evil, you make good that evil will spread.

Good guys look bad when bad guys look good.

When villains get rewarded, nations get contorted.

Progressives deform goodness rather than conform to goodness, and instead of converting religious people, they pervert religious people.

The distorted distort.

Demagoguery

Before they become the good guy, *demagogues* make someone else the bad guy.

Influence

Wisdom without clout does not shout. [24]

Not all men of renown are known.

The rich and famous are not the only ones with power. If you can influence someone influential, you can influence the world.

A person dies when their influence dies.

Service

If you want to be happy, serve yourself; if you want to make someone else happy, serve others.

The Great Commission

There is no greater mission than the Great Commission. [25]

The harvest workers work one harvest. [26]

Help and Assistance

To help the helpers is to help the helpless.

No single person can help every single person.

When God puts someone in your path, do whatever you can to get them on the right path.

Admission of Fault

Men who admit they are wrong need to be applauded, and those who refuse to admit others are right ought not to be lauded.

Make no mistake, he who admits to mistakes is never mistaken.

Zealotry and Extremism

The fundamentals of *fundamentalists* are not always fundamentally wrong.

Zealotry is good if it is for a good cause.

Extremism is entirely relative; Antarctic penguins are not cold at fifteen below, and Saharan camels are not hot at one hundred above.

Perception

Perceptions mold opinions.

Scales

Absolute attitudes require absolute altitudes.

Diverse scales cannot be scaled.

The absurd is heard every time scales are scaled back.

Bias

Pure objectivity is a rarity.

News and shoes are subject to tailoring.

Biased people avoid sparking flames because they know flames become fires, and fires burn ideologies to the ground.

Agendas

Wherever agendas are present, information is missing.

Professors and oppressors are suppressors of truth.

If a free press is not maintained for long, freedom cannot be obtained for long.

Freedom gets stressed every time agendas get pressed.

The Unseen Factor

A punch not seen is a punch not ducked.

To not know the one who is feeding is to not know the one who is leading.

Puppet masters master all.

Do not be fooled by someone who appears foolish; numbness is conceived when dumbness is perceived.

Danger beneath the nose knows nobody knows.

The enemy beyond your door is worse than the enemy beyond your shore.

Before you have a clue, the unseen enemy will have you.

Plots

An evil doctor had a patient on life support. The doctor wanted to pull the plug immediately, despite the wishes of the patient and his family. The only thing that stopped him was the wrath he would face if he did so.

The evil doctor was deceptive; he told the family it was his inclination to keep the patient alive, but in fact he had no intention of doing that. Instead, he slowly turned the power down so the patient would die without anyone noticing.

This is the explanation of the parable: the evil doctor represents *progressives*, the patient represents the rule of law, the life support system represents a constitution, and the patient's family represents the people of a republic.

Progressives know backlashes from the public will ensue if their real aims are ever brought to light; that is why they look like they are doing good when, in fact, they are doing evil. They also know citizens are more likely to be passive if they think their leaders are upright.

If *progressives* are to ever succeed in that they will have destroyed the rule of law, they will have done so by weakening its foundation first.

Seams split when schemes hit.

Forgotten Threats

A shepherd was tending his sheep. First, he saw a coyote approaching; then, two wolves drew his attention, and finally, three bears alarmed him. While the shepherd was watching the three bears, the three canine predators made a pact, and they devoured the shepherd's flock.

This is the explanation of the parable: the shepherd represents the public, the sheep represent the public's interests, the coyote represents a problem, the two wolves represent a bigger problem, and the three bears represent a huge problem.

The public gets itself in trouble whenever it takes its eye off the ball; old problems get replaced by new ones, and focuses get shifted; yesterday's forgotten problem can quickly become tomorrow's greatest threat.

Technology

Technology is not moral or immoral; it is neither good nor is it bad; it can make men happy, and it can make men sad.

Do not let your gadgetry become your *Idolatry*.

Use technology, but never let it use you.

He who controls machinery controls humanity.

Dangerous technology in the hand of an *imp* is like a loaded revolver in the hand of a chimp.

The Herd

Those easily marked are easy marks, and those hard to find are hard to bind.

Scattered birds and shattered sherds are difficult to herd.

Simple identification leads to simple annihilation.

Some sheep allowed themselves to be tagged. The rancher who kept them could pick them out easily for slaughter because they allowed him. The sheep were eventually rounded up after they received marks, and the rancher killed them one by one without so much as a struggle.

This is the explanation of the parable: the sheep represent individuals who do not mind being catalogued, and the rancher represents those doing the cataloguing.

Once you are identified, you can be crucified. The only way to stop evil-doers from herding is to not go along with the herd. If need be, do what is uncomfortable to avoid a holocaust; the discomfort you will feel is nothing compared to what you will feel after you are under complete control.

Before they go harshly into some bad plight, men always go gently into that good night.

Unhealthy Spirits

Only God can break a broken spirit.

Empty spirits are full of anguish.

Bodies ail after spirits fail.

Completeness

The whole conclusion: God makes whole.

The complete are completely God's.

Liberation

Men are liberators, but God liberates.

Dissatisfaction

The soul is never satisfied if the body is always gratified.

Worry

A heavy heart weighs down the mind, [27] and a broken mind breaks the body. [28]

Fewer worries bring fewer scurries to the hospital.

Big worries, little rest

Vexation halts relaxation.

Rest

A good night's sleep makes for a good day's work.

Vigor is needed for rigor.

People are at their best when they get at least eight hours rest.

Spirits and gadgets need charging.

Exhaustion

Strained men become drained men.

Unfilled tanks are filled with angst.

Little sleeping brings much weeping.

Early to rise and late to bed makes a man crabby, flabby, and dead.

Healthy Minds

Better to have a sound mind than to have a mound of cash, and living good and dying early is better than living long and dying surly.

CHAPTER 5

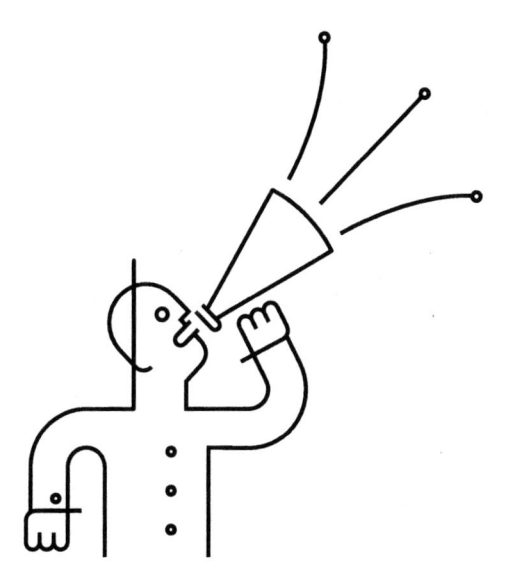

Science & Philosophy

Existence

I am, therefore I think.

Nothing causes nothing, some things cause some things, and everything (God) caused everything. Something cannot cause everything; every effect has a cause, and an effect cannot be its own cause. Something which is a result cannot result itself. The existence of the natural is evidence for the supernatural;[1] either life always existed, or it could have never existed.

It is unnatural for something natural to produce something supernatural. [1]

Existence is the greatest miracle of all.

If the probability of an event is zero, that means in all probability, the event probably never happened.

Order and Complexity

The order of disorder is chaos.

Wherever order exists, intelligence exists also.

Where there is information, there is an informer.

Covert complexity is the mark of overt simplicity.

God's finger left a fingerprint. [2]

It takes more faith to believe the universe was created by nothing than by an infinite God.

Singularity

Science is a tool for determining causes, the scientific method works by reading patterns, patterns repeat, and scientists cannot determine the cause of the universe scientifically because the cosmos was only created once—the act has not since been repeated.

The *Big Bang* bangs the idea the universe always existed.

Pluralistic universes do not have *singularities*.

Rationalism

The rationale for *Rationalism* is irrational.

The *Age of Reason* lacks reason because pure reason is not reasonable.

The *Enlightenment* enlightened the world to darkness.

Presupposition

Bargains not sought are never bought, and ideas which go uninspected go undetected.

Never throw out any hypothesis without testing it first. If you rule out any possibility, you might as well rule out every possibility.

Ideas get confected when logic gets rejected.

When truth gets muddied, facts get muddled.

Presupposed ideals produce presupposed ideas.

Whilst science is in the business of selling, it does not matter which case is more compelling.

It is easy to poke holes in pigeonholed science.

Context

Anything lacking context is just a pretext.

Philosophy

Philosophy is the lattice from which science draws its credence.

The difference between science and philosophy: science attempts to answer the how questions, and philosophy the why questions.

The difference between sound and unsound philosophy: good philosophy justifies itself, bad philosophy justifies the philosopher.

The difference between physics and *metaphysics*: physics helps to understand the laws of the universe; *metaphysics* helps to understand universal law.

Naturalism

Perfect circles and perfect explanations do not occur in nature.

Knowing nature and the nature of knowing are two separate things.

Scientists look for causes everywhere, and *Naturalists* only in the natural.

Modern science is really *Scientism*; by its nature it is *Naturalism*.

Scientism

Science was a method for questioning; now, it is a dogma not to be questioned.

Science combined with fiction is nothing more than science fiction.

Fancy for the fanciful is clemency for the fictional.

Anything subjective is susceptive.

Scientists who fail to acknowledge the limits of science fail to limit their own scientific acknowledgements.

When science becomes a god, science becomes a fraud.

Science and Religion

If you believe secular governments do not sponsor religion, you are mistaken. The *theory of evolution* is a religion,[3] and it is sponsored by secular governments throughout the world.

Atheistic theories are not necessarily scientific, and theistic theories are not necessarily unscientific.

Just because something is claimed to be secular does not mean it does not have religious claims.

Natural *secularism* is unnaturally religious.

Impure religion is purely religious, but religion based on fact is factually virtuous.

Evolution

Nature does not evolve naturally.

Which came first, *nature* or natural evolution?

Intelligence takes precedence, and *agency* is needed for *ascendancy*.

In science, the facts make the case, but in *evolution*, the case makes the facts.

The fossil record is a record against *evolution*. [4]

For if the fossil record shows *stasis*, the *theory of evolution* has no basis.

Transformational arguments exist within the contemporary record because *transitional forms* lack within the fossil record.

Only *fossils* believe the fossil record supports *evolution*.

The *Cambrian Explosion* explodes the *theory of evolution*.

Irreducible complexity and *specified complexity* spell complexity for *Darwinism*.

What came first, the cell or the DNA?

If creatures do not have the goods to survive, the odds are not good they will.

Mutations tend to mutilate rather than cultivate.

Beneficial mutations are like transcontinental relations; they occur, but they are not the norm.

Microevolution is observed in nature; *macroevolution* is only observed in the minds of *evolutionists*.

Creatures remain after their kind [5] even after a million years.

Once a chicken, always a chicken

Organisms that share common ancestors can reproduce. For example, horses and donkeys breed mules, lions and tigers generate ligers, and cattle and buffalo produce beefalo, but you will never see a man and a bat form a batman.

A finch can evolve a new beak, but a beak cannot evolve a new finch.

Evolutionists will not adapt to the fact that *adaptations* do not produce whole new *phylums*.

In the distant past there were more life forms on earth than today; most died off, [6] many adapted, and some are virtually unchanged, but there is no evidence to suggest any of the life forms evolved into entirely new creatures.

God did not have to reinvent the wheel every time He wheeled out a brand new life form.

Similar features make similar creatures.

Single designers produce single designs.

Differences make all the difference.

The *anthropic principle* principally opposes Darwin's claims.

Creationism is the enemy of scientists, not science.

Evolutionists believe in *natural selection* when it comes to *Darwinism*, but when it comes down to which theory is the fittest, *creation* or *evolution*, they do not. Theories besides the *theory of evolution* are not even considered by educators, and established scientific bodies dismiss theistic hypotheses outright as heresy. The *Creation* vs. *Evolution* debate will not evolve, at least not in an academic sense, as long as free intellectual discussions are hampered by a mammoth wall of pretense.

The *alien astronaut theory* is evidence that *evolutionists* have failed. The list is widening, and fewer people now believe human beings evolved from primordial life forms. Some *evolutionists* even admit the data is at odds with natural evolution and is more in line with creation, [4] but to maintain their naturalist worldview, it appears as if *evolutionists* now seek to replace the Creator God with little green men from another planet.

Theorists who cannot alternate universal reality alternate universes.

Science & Philosophy   111

Alternative universe is the universal alternative to *Evolution*.

Multiple universe theory multiplies folly.

Evolutionists do not believe pigs can fly, but they do believe pigs flew into existence through random processes.

Which is harder to believe, animals repopulated lands after a great flood, or all life forms emerged from *primordial ooze*? Animals repopulating lands sounds more plausible; animals are designed for the task, but ooze has no such innate capability.

Those who wanted to get *laid* laid the ground for *evolution*.[7]

The *theory of evolution* evolved from moral devolution.

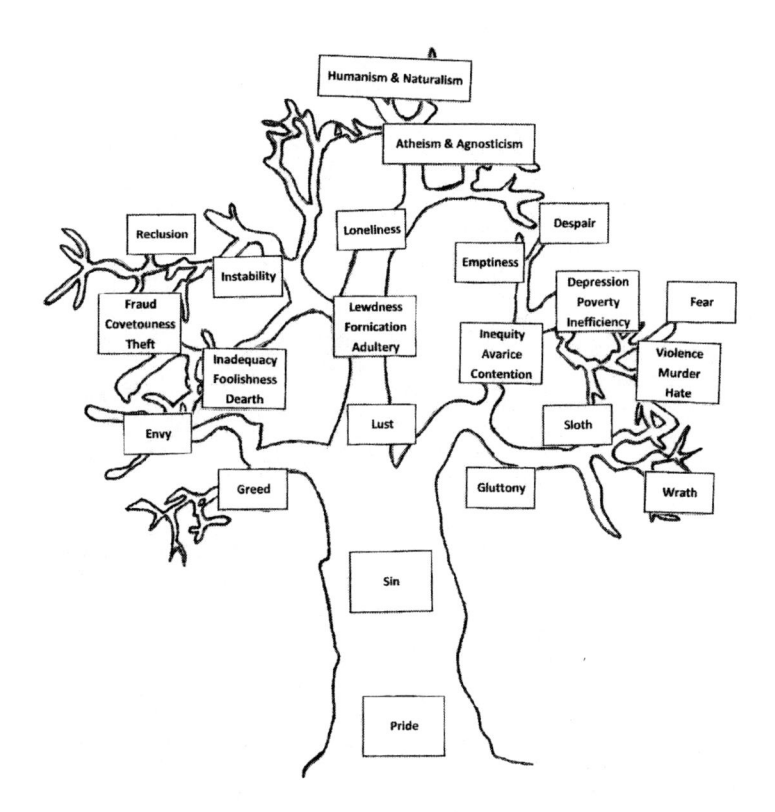

Animals do not evolve into men when God is absent; rather, men evolve into animals.

Animal farms farm animals.

Which is it, do apes act like men, or do men act like apes?

Any marriage between *Evolution* and *Creation* always ends in divorce.

Uniformitarianism

Uniformitarianism is uniformly questionable.

Assumptions generate assumed answers.

Variables vary things, and rate of change changes everything.

Anomalies are homilies.

Without *empirical* verification, it is hard to determine whether or not constants constantly adjust.

Until you can confirm everything, you cannot concede anything.

Uniformitarianism applies more to human beings.

Prophecy is frequently found in history.

As it was, it will always be.[8] Tomorrow's headlines are found in yesterday's history. What has already happened in the past will undoubtedly happen again in the future.

The future is set in stone as long as human beings remain as stubborn as a rock.

The same seed brings forth the same harvest.

Things never change, they just rearrange.

Uncertainty

Chaos does not exist, only unknowns.

If the *Heisenberg Uncertainty Principle* is really certain, then it is really uncertain.

Chance

Chances and dances are favorable when each and every step is known.

Forces

To know every force is to know every result.

The world is comprised of forces. The only thing that can stop a great force is an even greater force.

Space-Time Continuum

Time is a function of distance and rate of speed. To change time, the relationship between matter and space has to change.

Finite time travel into the future is a constant; objects are always moving from the past into the future. If you move faster than the speed of light, duration does not change; the only thing that changes is your position in space in relation to objects moving at a different rate. [9]

A single finite object cannot coexist with itself. Unless matter can be created or predated again, backward time travel is impossible in a dimensionally restricted environment.

The world will change, but it will never end. [10]

114   *Useful Maxims*

At the end of time, the past will not be remembered because the end of time is the beginning of time; we will have gone full circle. [11]

Time is a journey back to timelessness.

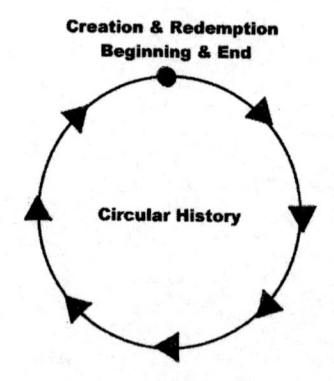

Creation & Redemption
Beginning & End

Circular History

CHAPTER 6

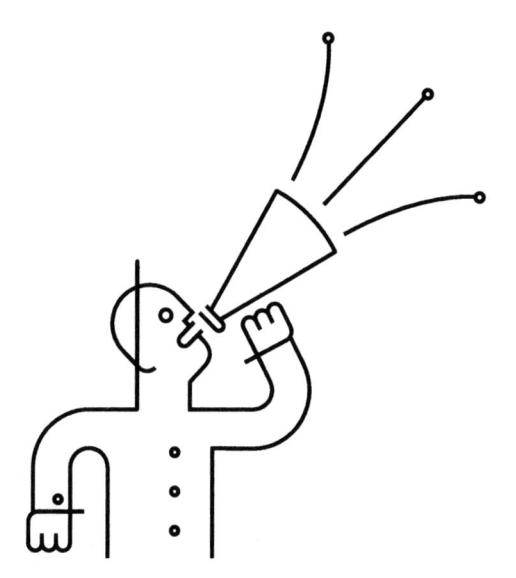

Evil, Suffering, & Judgment

Evil's Attributes

Nothing is inherently evil.[1] Evil becomes evil when it rebels against God.[2]

Before evil can dominate, it must germinate; it has to take root before it takes over.

Evil abounds on fertile grounds.

Evil is chilling when someone is willing.

Though evil may come over, it will never overcome.

Evil cuts until it is cut off.

Evil's ultimate triumph spells evil's ultimate defeat. [3]

Evil threatens when it becomes threatened.

Evil which is possible is probable.

Evil Worlds

After the godless get what they want, they do not want what they get.

A godless world is a joyless world. [4]

All is rotten after God is forgotten, [5] and all goes sour that is under satanic power. [6]

The Rise of Evil

It is easier for evil to ascend than for good to offend.

Everything gets seared once evil is feared.

Evil does well when the wicked swell, and when it is in dread, it does not spread.

Evil goes on when it goes unpunished. [7]

Evil is supported when it is not opposed.

Evil not attended is evil not contended.

People who do not stand in the way of evil stand to have evil in their way.

Evil breeds where evil feeds.

Evil gets hastened whenever good gets chastened.

Evil on the Run

The land cheers when evil fears.

Evil pursued cannot pursue.

That which is put to flight cannot fight.

Evil at bay finds no way.

Allowing Evil

Allowing evil to continue is the most evil act of all.

Evil's Presence

Good cannot exist without evil, for in the absence of evil, there is no faith; if faith is gone, there is no way to please God. [8] Righteousness is unattainable unless evil is present, because without evil, men cannot choose good over evil. Evil—as miserable as it is—actually yields uprightness. Evil is the vehicle by which God separates the sheep from the goats and the wheat from the tares. [9]

Evil dwells in men; [10] men do not dwell in evil.

If God doused evil, all of humanity would be destroyed in the process. Evil comes from the heart; [11] before it can be destroyed, it has to be purged; that is why God allows it to remain. [12] As long as evil lingers inside men's hearts, God will not destroy it before His work is done.

Man's Sinful Nature

God made everything good; [13] men make everything bad. [14]

Man's slavery to sin came out of free will.

Adam and Eve's descendants have no choice because Adam and Eve had one; as soon as they rebelled, corruption entered the world. [15]

Death

Death frees the curse. [16]

If the body did not die, it would live forever in a fallen state. [17]

Death only pains the living; pity the living, not the dead.

Suffering

To understand why something is, imagine for moment it was not.

Suffering is a buffering.

A little pain wards off a lot of pain, and temporal suffering prevents eternal suffering.

Man suffers pain because he does not suffer restraint.

How Evil Is Fought

Every time God is obeyed, the devil is wounded.

Evil is upended whenever virtue is defended, and it is destroyed if righteousness is deployed.

Once evil is *blighted*, civilizations get righted.

God comes to you when you avoid evil, and when you come to God, evil avoids you.

The Devil and Devils

Satan was the first to sin, [18] and he will be the last to enter the *Lake of Fire*. [19]

Satan's time is short; [20] if you align yourself with him, your time will be short as well.

Satan is no threat to God, [21] he is a threat to man. He is not God's adversary, he is man's adversary. [22]

Vices are the devil's devices.

The devil cannot make you do anything; he just makes you believe you can do anything.

The *Fallen Angel* caused man's fall. [23]

Lucifer is as crafty as he is evil. If the devil appeared hideous, nobody would be attracted to him. *Satan* is too shrewd to reveal himself; he draws men close by pretending to be something he is not. [24] Many fall prey to him because they are unable to spot him. The way to spot *Satan* is to know Christ.

A snake which cannot charm you is a snake which cannot harm you.

Satan's lies do harm when they are accepted as truth.

Those girded with truth are hard targets for *Satan*. He can shoot his fiery arrows at them, but they do not penetrate truth's armor. Once *Satan* realizes he can no longer deceive, he gives up. [25] *Satan* is not to be feared, he is to be avoided.

Stay away from the *Wicked One*, and the *Wicked One* will stay away. [26]

Devils are more afraid of God [27] than they are fearsome.

Devils are not sovereign like God; they do not have power to create, and they cannot destroy without God's permission. However, devils drive people crazy with their incessant buzzing, and people destroy themselves because of it.

Systematic Evil

Anything tied to evil is tied by evil.

Systematic evil ties systematically.

Pure and Impure Evil

Better to be on the bad side of good than to be on the good side of bad.

Pure evil kills fast and to the core; impure evil kills slowly, but it kills much more.

That which is infected is deadlier than that which is rejected.

A man only eats things which are treats.

Evil which appears godly is the most insidious form of evil.

The Occult

Do not look for God in the *occult*; all you will find are *occult* gods.

There is nothing new about the *New Age Religion*; the *New Age Religion* is just the *old age religion* in a different skin. Do not be deceived by old, dark demons masquerading themselves as fresh new beings of light. Today's spiritualism is no different than yesterday's *paganism*; it is repackaged evil from way back, retooled for a modern contemporary audience.

There is no such thing as a good witch.

Do not dabble with devils; if you mess with the *occult*, the *occult* will mess with your mind.

Sorcery is a source of misery.

False Religion

Hungry souls are not fed by starving beliefs.

Ungodly religion does not provide godly provision. [28]

An evil weed from an evil seed can never feed one's deepest need.

Bad instruments cannot play good music.

Idols and rifles backfire.

Evil Partaken

Houses are shaken when evil is partaken.

Redefined Evil

Evil redefined becomes realigned.

Evildoers

Anyone anti-Christ is an antichrist. [29]

Devilish men are devils with flesh.

The difference between evil spirits and evil men: evil spirits know they are dead, [30] and evil men are dead because they do not know. [31]

After they lose control, evildoers lose composure.

Exercised demons exercise opposition.

Those who do evil and think it is well, unknowingly take everyone on a long trip to hell.

Judgment

Our own words are our own judge. [32]

The words Jesus Christ spoke speak judgment. [33]

Salvation and Damnation

The good may die young, but the young never die good. [34]

The *dead in Christ* only die once. [35]

The longsuffering do not suffer for long, and the *quickened* recover quickly.

Those written in the *Book of Life* are booked for life. [36]

Those appointed with God are not appointed to wrath. [37]

You are damned if you do not receive salvation, and you are not damned if do. [38]

Those seated next to Christ on His throne [39] will not stand before the *Great White Throne*.

Those who fail to live up to God's standard fail to live. [40]

Propitiation is needed for redemption. [41]

It is man's decision whether or not he wants perdition.

Who we serve determines where we end up.

Men go to hell when they go astray.

When God is rejected, hell is selected.

To be abandoned, one must abandon salvation.

Only those who will salvation will be saved.

Heaven and Hell

Heaven is not a reward for being good, and hell is not a punishment for being bad. We go to heaven for being like Christ, and we go to hell for being like ourselves. It is not what a man does that lands him in hell, it is what he does not do that sends him there. If you do not want to be in hell, then be in Christ Jesus; open the door when the Lord comes knocking, and the gates of hell will not be opened when death comes marching.

Hell is a temporary place for the depraved, and heaven is an eternal place for the saved. In the dispensation of time, those already condemned [38] will be poured into the *Lake of Fire*, and those predestined for life [42] will receive every bit of God's desire.

Hell is a dark place where God's light does not shine and where the hope of His salvation is at the end of its line.

Battling Evil

Turning the other cheek [43] does not mean turning a blind eye. [44]

Resist evil, but resist it with good and not with evil. [45]

When evil fights evil, evil always wins.

To wrong evil is to right evil.

Natural weapons do not affect supernatural foes; a mighty gun will not harm an evil ghost.

CHAPTER 7

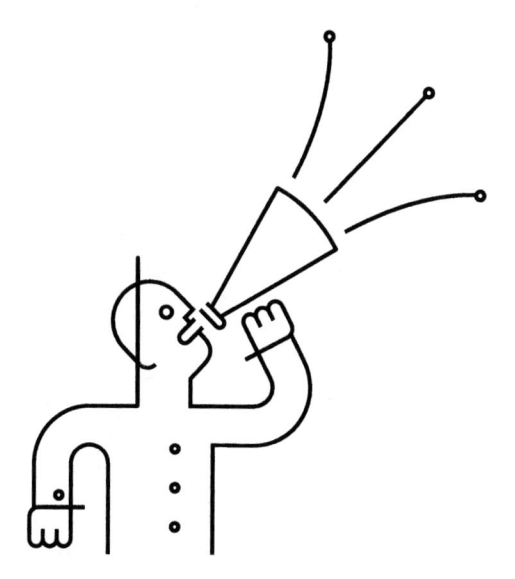

Economics

Patience

Fruit picked too early tastes sour.

Stew always tastes better after it simmers.

If you want everything now, you will have nothing later.

Sacrifice today and you will have what you need tomorrow.

Huge towers are built one small brick at time.

The Rush to Be Rich

What is built quickly falls quickly, and what takes no time to build tumbles in no time. [1]

Quick bucks go out just as quick as they come in.

The rush to be rich hastens poverty. [2]

Evaporation of Wealth

Wantonness leaves men in want.

Mammon, like salmon, makes its way upstream and then dies.

Vanity vanishes. [3]

Money is like honey until it becomes runny.

Emotions run high until finances run dry.

Avarice

Avarice is never satisfied. [4]

Desire always reaches higher. [5]

An insatiable beast never has enough upon which to feast.

Cupidity leads to stupidity.

Materialism

There is more to life than getting more in life.

Worldly men and hungry fish are attracted to shiny objects.

Materialist dreams never materialize.

Satisfaction from things does not satisfy a thing.

Endless holes do not help hapless souls, and useless gifts do not fill godless rifts.

Much does little for those with little much.

Plenty does not satisfy pity.

Consumerism

Do not be consumed by *consumerism*.

Vain Endeavors

Health yields to wealth, and happiness capitulates to capital.

The quest for much is much for nothing.

The vain strain for naught.

From the treasures of wickedness come measures of insipidness.

Notice the man who loves money more than right: everything which he has built will eventually take flight. [6]

Using money wisely is beneficial; using it poorly is sacrificial.

Builders of vanity labor in vain. [7]

Profits of iniquity profit no one. [8]

Ungodly fruit becomes godly loot. [9]

Gluttony

Insatiability is the road to insufficiency.

Gluttony leads to poverty.

Before you add more pain, make sure you can bear the strain, or else everything you acquire will certainly expire as your financial house of cards comes crashing down in a great economic fire.

The fat man becomes a lean man when the fat man is not a keen man.

Do not be a greedy man, and you will not end up a needy man.

Better to tighten a little than to loosen it all.

A little bit of money is better than no money.

The difference between *sloths* and gluttons: a *sloth* does nothing to supply his own needs, and a glutton does everything to need everyone's supply.

The greedy horde brings forth the *feudal lord*, and a *feudal fief* draws in the *communist* thief.

Gleaning

Locusts devour fields until they die of starvation; likewise, greedy men buy up property until there is great *Stagflation*.

All is lean after all men glean.

He who overruns his supply has his supply overran.

Prosperity

Before you can do well, you must do penance.

Piety is the key to prosperity.

Obedience is a prime ingredient for success.

All is for the taking if you obey God above all.

Increase cometh when offense leaveth.

Life is more pleasurable when sin is less measurable.

Work Ethic

Do for duty and not for *booty*.

Better to have God's commendation than to have man's compensation.

Jobs which are done correctly never have to be corrected.

The man who is always in demand never lacks cash within his hand.

A job well done does well to secure one's job.

People receive unemployment settlements when all they seek are employment benefits.

If you spend all your time worrying about your job and no time working, it is just a matter of time before you will be spending time looking for a new one.

Stable work and able workers are hard to find.

The self-employed are always employed.

Poor Management

Administrators who are not grounded run institutions to the ground.

Practices are only as strong as their weakest practitioners.

When the *ivory tower* fumbles, the entire kingdom crumbles.

Cheapness

As water sinks to the lowest point on land, consumers go wherever they can land the cheapest price.

Cheap labor is not cheap; it cheapens economies.

Outsourcing

Slavery is demanded whenever a demand for slaves is created.

When the land of opportunity becomes a trough for opportunists, the opportunities leave.

Purchasing Power

No money means no power, and little money means little option.

When increase outpaces income, people get left behind.

Purchasing power purchases power.

Short-sidedness

Cutting the workforce cuts into stability. Businesses do not remain afloat very long after too many people are laid off. The economy works when people work; money has to be made before it can be spent. Strategies that keep people working are the best strategies for long-lasting economic strength.

Short-sided business plans plan for long-term failure.

Labor

Before wealth can be redistributed, it has to be created, and unless there are incentives to work, work will not take place.

Labor occurs when labor produces.

Shaky Ground

Economic *alchemy* leads to political calamity.

Much brutality follows little frugality.

Anything not founded upon God fundamentally lacks foundation. [10]

That which is built on nothing has nothing supporting it.

Much dies where little lies.

False securities secure true fatalities.

Weak sutures make for bleak futures.

Things that are frail can fail.

People ache after safety nets break.

Those who trust vanity are entrusted to vanity.[11]

Ponzi schemes scheme the pawns.

Economic bubbles make economic troubles.

Before becoming vested, make sure it is tested.

Tried and True Practices

Good traditions are good foundations.

Often, the best way to tackle the future is to revert to the past.

What has always worked will always work.

Throwbacks throw conditions back on track.

Efficiency

Before you can surge, you must purge.

Cut the fat before the fat cuts your throat.

Unburned *chaff* burns the staff.

Clean operations are lean operations, and efficient men are rarely deficient men.

Groundwork

Groundwork sets up sound work.

Prepared men are not impaired men.

Consequence

Good economic decisions make good economic times, for the economy grows when foolishness slows.

Dearth cometh when earth sinneth.

Purses are thin when curses are thick.

Tears of tribulation follow years of emasculation.

Decades of decadence precede cascades of impediments.

Sinful ways go before painful days.

Unethical traditions bring forth unbearable conditions.

Awful *norms* brew dreadful storms.

Errors bring terrors.

Socialism

Fat governments make lean wallets.

Government benefits from *socialism*, not the consumer.

Communism only works when it is not worked into the economy.

Sooner or later, *federal* states become *feudal* estates.

All states are *lavatories* when no states are laboratories.

Economic Philosophy

Barriers to entry are barricades against economic growth.

The economy expands when *potential energy* is allowed to become *kinetic energy*.

The Invisible Hand [12] cannot drive the economy in the right direction if it is severed from the arm.

Supply and Demand supplies a demand for innovation.

Laissez-Faire is not for the fairly lazy.

Government Intervention

Economies on life support should be unplugged.

The *phoenix* ascends after fire descends.

Unlimited intervention limits the market's ability to intervene.

Aided recoveries are jaded recoveries.

Long concessions extend brief recessions.

Economies

Economies are like forests; they experience growth and decline, and sometimes, they undergo catastrophe. The key? Do not hinder the forest. Let it recuperate naturally. If *bureaucrats* stay out of the way, economies eventually right themselves.

Carrion feeders allow economies to carry on.

The economic cycle is like a bouncing ball; forces affect its trajectory. No matter how good the boom, gravity ultimately pulls every economy back to the ground, and no matter how bad the recession, economies rebound when they can sink no further. Finally, inertia keeps economies moving upward if they have enough energy, until gravity pulls them down again.

Economies are like rockets; they need fuel, and they require capital and investment; otherwise, they do not move. Also, auxiliary fuels like savings are important so when profits dry up, secondary burns keep the economy aloft.

Economies are fueled by need, not by greed.

Demagogues show up whenever economies slow down.

So many variables and so few verities is precisely what sinks so many economies.

Economic Systems

Broken people break down systems.

Capitalism is as good or as bad as those who utilize it.

Crony capitalism is phony *capitalism*.

Saving

It is good to have additional cash whenever there is an inhospitable crash.

Only men who build arks survive financial floods.

Saving money is making money.

What you keep in your bank is reserve in your tank.

Hedging

One tree has one chance for fruit, but many trees have many chances.

Sow more than one plant for more than one yield.

They go over the ledge who do not hedge.

Planting

Evil seeds produce evil weeds. [13]

Do not expect to reap wheat if you sow tares.

An egg hatches what an egg clutches. [13]

If you want a different harvest, then sow a different seed.

Money

Dollars are soldiers; deploy them, never destroy them.

Money will not help a *whelp*.

Making money is not evil, making it your god is. [14]

Conservation

Today's discretion builds tomorrow's surplus.

If you want to be rich, then act poor.

Be a good steward of your resources; what you preserve today will be there for you tomorrow.

Land protection lands protection.

Short-sidedness creates shortages.

Keep your hands from your pocket if you cannot keep yourself from spending.

It is wiser to be a *miser* than to be in the poorhouse.

The *miser* has less misery than his brother in poverty.

Before, poor men lacked bread; today, they lack restraint.

Yield

It is not what you make but what you keep, and where you are matters less than where you end up.

Easy Fortunes

Where there are ditches, do not expect to find riches.

Heaps of cash are not found in heaps of trash.

Covetousness

He who always wants money is always in want of money.

Covetous men rarely have anything worth coveting.

Enterprise

Making money is the principal goal of fools.

Being poor is the ultimate end, if being rich is the ultimate goal.

The itch to be rich does not stitch.

Products merit money; money does not merit products.

Great ideas generate great recompense.

Financial success is achieved through steadfastness, not avariciousness.

Perspirations, not aspirations, create wealth.

Excellence is achieved through vigilance.

Initiative

With little strain comes much pain.

You cannot reap fruit if you do not sow seed.

Before a man can earn a life, he must learn to live.

Waking up is the first step to making any dream a reality.

Ability lends to stability, and readiness makes *ruddiness*.

Accomplished missions accomplish victory.

Drive drives men further.

A man without motivation is like a ship without navigation.

Seekers of pleasure lack treasure because they are always after leisure.

Contentment

Living within your means is the best means to rid financial stress.

To decrease content is to increase lament.

Be content with what you have, or you will have a lot to contend with.

God knows what is needed; [15] we need to know what is seeded.

Accumulation

Unmanageable increase manages to increase sorrows.

Exuberance and affluence are not synonymous.

Opulence leads to *corpulence*.

Wealthy men are not always healthy men.

Men with a lot have a lot to worry about. [16]

Huge houses require huge bank accounts.

To have every piece is to never have peace. [16]

The more we have, the more we have to maintain. [17]

The man who owns it all owes it all.

With accumulation comes obligation.

Mortgages and Homes

Home ownership is not authentic until deed ownership is authenticated.

Fully abided abodes are fully paid off.

Steadfast men remain fast in their stead.

Buy houses for long-term dwelling, not for short-term selling.

Financing

If you are being enriched by someone else's money, you are making someone else even richer while making yourself a *serf*.

Financing what you need is not greed, but financing what you crave only makes you a slave.

Possessions

It is hard to hold on to what you own if you do not own what you have.

Possess your possessions, but never allow them to possess you.

Possessions breed obsessions, and obsessions spawn transgressions.

Prosperity plus iniquity equals calamity.

Value

Anything with value has a price, something no one will pay for has no value, and something no one can pay for has no price.

Goodness is not purchased with goods, and *tender* does not provide tenderness. [18]

Godliness exceeds loftiness. [19]

A pence of dignity is worth more than an ounce of gold.

Usury

Users use *usury*.

Any interest you give to a lender is capital you do not take for yourself.

Excessive interest is in the interest of those who love excess.

Debt

Insurmountable debt surmounts any chance at freedom.

Being under arduous debt is like swimming across an ocean with a heavy stone tied to your ankle; you can stay afloat while you are in the shallows, but once you are in deep water, that debt will pull you down into the abyss.

A prince was told he would be king. This prince lived excessively until the day his father died because he believed it was his right to become king. He acquired land and other goods and made agreements as if he was already ruler.

The prince did not know his mother the queen already made arrangements for his brother to become king. When the time had come for the new king to take his seat, the prince saw someone else sitting on the throne. To say the least, the prince was distraught; he was left holding debt without any means of paying it off.

The prince is likened to a fool who believes he has some sort of right to income and that his financial situation will never change. When people assume the best and do not prepare for the worst, that is when they get caught with their pants down. Be ready for the most awful situation, and you will be set for any situation.

A group of partiers rented a hotel room to throw a bash. The room was pristine before the partiers arrived, but by the time they left, it was destroyed. The bash lasted for hours, alcohol was ordered, and nobody paid attention to the tab or the condition of the room.

The next morning, the hotel manager came into the room while the partiers were hung over, and he gave them their tab and a huge bill for the cleanup.

This is the explanation of the parable: the partiers represent people who live in the moment, the hotel room represents the economy, and the hotel manager represents banks and lenders.

People who live in the moment are always shocked whenever reality sets in; they live it up when times are good, but when the economy takes a turn for the worse, they are not prepared for what lies ahead. Banks and lenders will come for their money, that much is sure; think about that the next time you throw caution to the wind.

Debt economies are never set economies because they are always on the verge of becoming beset economies.

Credit economies lack credibility.

Big deficits, little hope

Rich and Poor

The difference between a rich man and a poor man: rich men have more than they need, and poor men need more than they have.

The difference between a rich man and a wealthy man: rich men spend to have much, and wealthy men have much to spend.

Those given much ought to give much back. [20]

Consumer Awareness

Never buy from someone who is willing to lie.

Bad companies are kept erect by good consumers who do not inspect.

Corporations cannot continue without a continual revenue stream.

CHAPTER 8

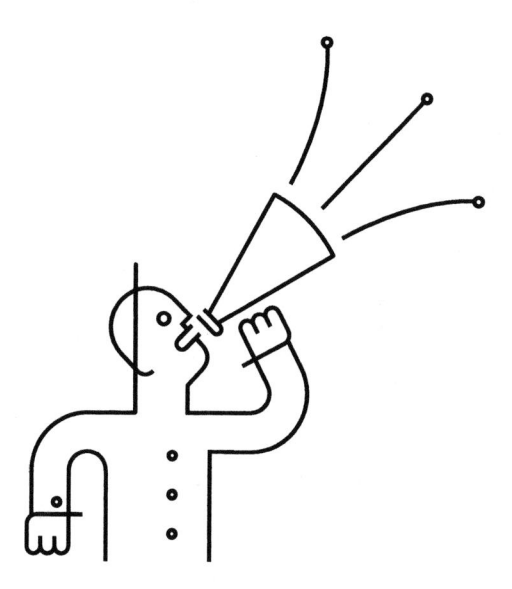

Law, Government, and Civics

Loss of Liberty

The dream loses its gleam before the dream loses its steam.

Nations lose virtue before they lose liberty.

If virtue gets wielded, liberty gets shielded.

When knowledge is aborted, freedom gets thwarted.

Temperance

Freedom without temperance is *anarchy*, and *anarchy* is the first step toward *tyranny*.

Those who govern themselves have no need of government, and men who seek saviors other than Jesus Christ seek their own demise.

Uncontrollability gives government the ability to control.

Restraint prevents constraint.

Big Government and Big Business

Anything too big to fail is too big to allow.

Powerful government hates losing power, and gainful business hates gaining competition.

Big government and big business are big problems, and big government plus big business equals big trouble.

Welfare for the rich is neither well nor fair.

Big corrupt governments who lecture big greedy corporations about ethical violations are much like *Satan* rebuking *Abaddon*.

Communism

Communism is not a cooperative.

Tyranny loves company.

The force of *socialism* is it is forced socially.

No *socialist* has ever achieved success without achieving successive control.

Whenever voids get filled with liberty, *communism* gets voided.

Systems under high pressure naturally move to areas of low pressure; likewise, civilizations under *autocracy* organically shift toward *autonomy*.

Communists promise freedom before they dispense enslavement.

Communism never completely disappears; it gets a completely new name whenever it gets completely exposed.

In the past *socialists* used tanks and soldiers to subdue others; today they use lawyers and judges.

Darwinistic evolution is the basis for communistic revolution.

The Origin of Species is the origin of *feces*.

Communists remove God in an attempt to become god.

Karl Marx and Friedrich Engels were not the first *communists*; they were the founders of *Marxism*, but not *communism*. *Communism* dates further back than the nineteenth century. The first group of *communists* dwelt in the land of *Shinar*; these *communists* tried to make a name for themselves by building a tower reaching up to heaven. They failed.[1] *Communism* continued and still continues to this day whether by *tribalism, imperialism, socialism*, or other collectivist ideologies.

Communism is not an economic or political system; it is a philosophy rooted in rebellion. Once people begin to think they are superior to God, *communism* takes root. Human beings are creatures made to worship God; it is in the nature of man to serve the Almighty. When we reject the living God and His commandments, we create a dilemma; we need God and His laws; we merely create a vacuum in need of filling. Unfortunately, evil is always ready to step in whenever God is removed from the equation; either man has to become his own god, or he must serve false gods. In either case, evil obtains a foothold.

To free yourself from God is to enslave yourself to man.

Once the Creator is gone, danger is spawn.

Communism thrives where godliness dives, for *Marxism* defeats wherever *Christianity* retreats.

The *New World Order* repeats the old world error. [2]

Nimrods emulate *Nimrod*.

If it is not God's will, it is the devil's.

Men who think they can be like God are more like *Lucifer*. [3]

Evil desires make evil empires.

The quest for supremacy raises the threat of *tyranny*.

Utopias and unicorns do not exist.

Man's plan for peace is a piece of dung. [4]

Checks and Balances

All hangs in the balance without checks and balances.

Checks and balances keep evil in check.

Lost Generations

Wherever *youthful idealism* touts, *collectivism* sprouts.

Children decree when adults flee.

Generations that lose their children are followed by generations that lose their liberty.

The Silent Majority

A sleeping bear bears no prowess.

If the *Silent Majority* is silent the majority of the time, liberty will be silenced.

Much silence breeds much violence.

Minority Rule

The toothless must be ruthless.

If the weak want to rule the strong, they must make the strong think they are weak.

A large elephant was bound by a thin rope. The elephant made no attempt to break free because she thought the rope was too strong.

One day by accident the elephant shifted her weight, and she broke the rope with ease. After the zookeepers saw the severed rope, they fled, and the elephant marched off to freedom.

This is the explanation of the parable: the large elephant represents moral majorities, the zookeepers represent small but well-organized status quo minorities, and the thin rope represents myths that hold back majorities.

The only grip a minority can hold over a majority is a psychological one. The majority has to be deceived for it to be controlled. Once a majority learns it has more power, the minority will have no choice but to flee, because the majority will trample it under foot.

When the rules are weak, the weak rule.

Vigilant minorities are more influential than complacent majorities.

Counterfeit Authority

That which feigns power drains power.

Fake authority fakes authority.

Small but Dangerous Cabals

Tenuous fakes are like venomous snakes. [5]

Tiny serpents deliver deadly poisons.

Toxicity makes up for fragility.

Without immunity, toxins kill with impunity.

Unrestricted Restrictions

With many laws comes little enforcement.

Cords of restriction are the swords of manipulation.

New laws destroy old liberties.

Gun control is the best way to suppress free people. When a citizenry can no longer defend itself, a despot's job becomes much easier. [6]

Sooner or later, restrictions that are voluntary become mandatory.

Rights that do not exist for many of us eventually become obsolete for all of us.

Options are taken before oppression is given.

Yokes and oaks branch out.

Neglect

If the people do not care, neither will their government.

Politicians pay no attention to people who pay no attention to them.

Neglected liberty becomes lost liberty, and uncherished liberty perishes.

Free societies are free to destroy their own freedoms.

Those given freedom to surrender, surrender freedom, and those given the right to ignore, ignore their rights.

Eugenics

Once government has the right to murder someone, it has the right to murder everyone.

Governments that decide who lives and who dies hold within their hand everyone's demise.

Babies are abhorred when their rights are ignored; a women's right is a baby's plight, for infants lose when mothers choose.

Killing the innocent kills innocence.

The common thread of all *eugenics*: all *eugenicists* hate commoners.

He who does not look up to his Father in heaven looks down upon his brother on earth.

Subjugation

Government takes power from the people when the people grant it undue powers.[7]

Government takes over when the people roll over.

Pushovers get pushed over.

Autocracy means automatic slavery.

After government takes over everything, it is difficult to do anything.

It is hard to get out from underneath an umbrella system.

It takes courage to a buck a system that systematically bucks.

When government controls the entire pie, the people must fight for every piece.

The subjugated are subjected to being subjects.

Political Strife

Power struggles strangle civility.

Politicians cannot abuse authority they do not have; if government's power is limited, leaders will not fight amongst themselves for more control.

Church and State

The "wall of separation between church and state" spoken of by Thomas Jefferson [8] separates the state from the church, not the church from the state.

In America the state cannot establish a religion, [9] but in every nation, a religion can establish the state.

Neutral governments do not exist; strict secular governments are nothing more than *atheocracies*.

A crucifix worn around someone's neck is less offensive than a government noose fastened around everyone's throat, and religious statues are less provocative than statutes that ban them.

Civility

Eye for an eye makes really good sense because it is really about recompense.

Established bars bar *barbarism*.

Restitution restores civility.

Breakdown of the Rule of Law

Civilizations unravel as soon as they unravel the rule of law. [10]

Economic and political situations improve, though once the rule of law has been tampered with, corruption is practically unavoidable.

Lawless governance of the body leads the way to flawless severance of the head.

Monarchies have monarchs, and *oligarchies* have oligarchs; *democracies* that abandon the rule of law are at the mercy of countless demogarchs.

Mob Tyranny

Tyranny is *tyranny*; to those under oppression, the number of *despots* is neither here nor there.

Tyranny of the mob and a mob of *tyranny* both mob the citizenry.

Demagogues derail *democracies*.

Law's Foundation

Unless man's law is God's law, man's law is futile.

Laws not resting upon something bigger than paper are not worth the paper they are written upon.

Laws are meaningless unless they emanate from a higher power.

Before any law can be founded, a foundation for every law must be established.

Unjust Balances

Wherever law is unpredictable, peace is unobtainable.

Wrested judgment creates unrest.[11]

Diverse scales tip justice off balance.

The Rule of Men

The person behind the bench ought not to be a *benchmark*.

When opinions become the law of the land, the land becomes subject to vanity, and when evil men judge, evil becomes law.

Corrupted Authority

Corrupt laws construct flaws.

Deceived judges cannot conceive judgment.

The unjust just undermine justice.

Respecters of persons [12] personally have no respect for law.

Legislation from the Bench

In case you did not know, *case law* creates law.

Courts courted by *Progressives* court disaster.

Lack of Justice

Nations immune from justice are immune to freedom.

Poor Government

Leadership which cannot govern itself should not govern at all.

Governments not in the business of governing have no business governing.

Better to be hardly governed than to be badly governed.

Power

The only thing that ensures freedom is power.

The buck stops at the *buckler*.

Power lies where power flies.

The scepter is heaved in upheaval.

Whoever has the last say says he is king.

Strengthen the natural law of men, and naturally, only the strongest men will survive.

Power sours even the noblest men.

Unless power is backed by God, it has no backing. [13]

Much power with little virtue brings much trouble with little hope.

People who do not take power seriously have their power seriously taken. [14]

Power that is not going to remain just, just is not going to remain.

What good is power if it does not do any good?

Stable Government

Order follows the following of *statutory law*.

Constructionists construct concord.

Those who hate authority berate stability.

Stable civilizations are built upon a strong covenant between the people and their government. The role of government is to protect the people from injustice, and the role of the people is to obey the law. Whenever either side breaks its agreement, the system no longer works.

Godly Disobedience

The Shepherd's sheep [15] ought not to be sheepish.

The powers that be are not always those seated in power; kings reign supreme in kingdoms, but in a *representative democracy*, the people are the authority. If their representatives are doing evil, or they are usurping control, the people not only have a right to resist them, it is their God-given duty to do so. [16]

Authorities that do not respect Ultimate Authority ultimately do not have to be respected. [17]

Awful dictators are seeded whenever unlawful dictates are heeded.

Government's Responsibility

Government is there to make peace; [18] it is not there to take every piece we make.

Free government is not supposed to guarantee any one person success, but that every person has the right to succeed.

Job creation is not government's job.

Good governments foster good environments.

Ungodly Nations

Governments that do not serve the good of the people are no good to the people, and governments that ignore God get ignored by God.

Nations are either under God or under threat.

Once a nation's hedge is gone, gone is that nation. [19]

Great powers that trash the Great God eventually end up on the trash heap of history.

Countries that forget God are soon forgotten.

When they do not call for mercy, nations fall from grace.

Rulers

Knowledge is ruled out in advance whenever rulers lack advanced knowledge.

When the state protects the people from oppression, you have a government serving the people, and when the state protects itself from the people, you have a government serving oppression.

Governments that lead everyone have everyone as leader.

He who pays the bills runs the mills.

They are kings who pull the strings.

When the many rest on the backs of the few, the few become rulers.

Bad leaders are led in, and poor rulers rule over the morally impoverished.

Political Slavery

The end to bravery marks the start to slavery.

Reliant men are compliant men.

Permanent constituencies are created by permanent dependencies.

The dependent are always deficient.

If you want to enslave a man, give him just enough to survive but not enough to prosper.

Crumbs are enough for those with a crumby existence.

Flattery goes before treachery, [20] and bribery makes slavery. [21]

Flattery and bribery are tools for mutiny.

People addicted to government do not resist government.

Only those with no master can say no.

Serfs and sieves do not hinder.

Entitlements enlist enslavements, and handouts hand out subjugation.

Political slavery makes everything unsavory.

Police states are prisons.

Free Money

Repercussions render reserve.

Free money is free from responsibility.

It is hard to lobby against those who lob money.

With much relaxation comes much taxation.

One man's security is another man's liability.

What is *pork* to some is payment for others.

To some, *bureaucrats* are zeros, and to others, they are heroes.

Taxes

Render unto *Caesar*,[22] but not unto *Satan*.[23]

Money wasted by government is money not put to good use by its earner.

He who is forced to give all to a whore has nothing left with which to feed the poor.

The practice of giving money out of the goodness of your heart to someone in need is called charity, and the practice of government taking money from your pocket out of duress and giving it to someone who will not work is called larceny.

The difference between giving and taxing: givers are willing participants, and taxers are stealing recipients.

Tax is the ax which cuts off *autonomy*.

God requires but a tenth of our *hire*;[24] government's desire is all we can sire.

When welfare pays more than employers, taxpayers pay the ultimate price.

Social Justice

Government programs that help the poor help everyone become poor.

Social justice justifies *socialism*.

The difference between religious and secular *Marxists*: the religious *Marxist* believes God is the state, and the secular *Marxist* believes the state is god.

Para-*socialists* and parasites need hosts to survive.

Accountability

The people must own up to *government ownership*.

Voters rain down opposition every time politicians rein in spending.

If their constituents do not curb their appetite for government programs, elected officials cannot curb the size of government.

Self-reliance

Followers never lead.

Do not let anyone do for you what you can do for yourself.

The back seat is not a good place from which to drive.

Take some initiative if you do not like where you are being taken.

Men fall into *thrall* when they do not stand on their own at all.

People who stand alone in life do not lie together in death.

He who protects himself is never far from protection.

Individual Action

Good decisions go much further than government intervention, little steps add up with each stride, and consistent action trumps great action.

Assumed actions assail *activism*.

Just doing the little things makes a huge difference.

Actions desired by everyone are required by no one.

Those well below their enemy's radar are far above their enemy's reproach.

Grassroots Insurgencies

Changed people change nations.

Depressed people depress peoples.

Despot leaders feed off desperate needers.

Domestication

The domesticated cannot be liberated.

Easiness kills readiness.

People at ease are easily herded.

The comfortable are conformable.

To love life is to hate strife.

The uncomfortable will fight, and the comfortable do not have the will to fight.

Political Despair

The will gets killed whenever the thrill gets chilled.

Those with nothing to fight for have everything to fight for.

Phony Politicians

Record trumps rhetoric.

Intimate associates reveal secret associations.

Character matters more than theatre.

Political spin is a tool to win.

The Democratic Process

Democracy does not guarantee *autonomy*.

It is just as easy to choose slavery as it is sovereignty.

With poor aims come sore chains.

Uninformed electorates advance unabashed *Confederates*.

People who vote their heart vote their death.

If your party abandons you, abandon it. Parties change; change your party if your party changes its platform and you no longer agree with it.

Do not caucus with evildoers if you do not want evildoers to cause raucous.

Send them packing who pack on new regulation.

Do not replace bad incumbents with good liars, and never exchange a dullard for a devil.

When options A and B look bad, choose option C, and if there is not an option C, make one.

The lesser of two evils is still evil.

Vote for policies, not people.

The democratic process becomes a demographic process whenever ethnicity and gender are the deciding factor.

Who are the bigger fools, foolish politicians or the fools who put them in office?

Crooked voters vote in crooked leaders.

The most honorable become the least electable when the least respectable become the most delectable.

Politicians do not mind mindless constituents.

Leadership

When their leaders have understanding, the people understand leadership.

Leaders involved in mischief miss the opportunity to remain chief.

Men enthralled with their throne will not remain enthroned to *thrall*.

He follows folly who leads poorly.

Polls

Some polls reflect, and others infect.

What is doled mostly depends on who is polled.

The majority feels left out whenever left out of the majority.

Dishonest polls are the result of dishonest pollsters.

Infiltration

Beware of individuals who organize, politicize, and illegitimize; their goal is to revolutionize.

The difference between organized and politicized labor: organized labor is supportive, and politicized labor is exploitive.

Infiltration is a lot easier than confrontation.

A wicked businessman bought a respectable factory. Before he acquired the plant, it was an honest establishment with a good product line, and because of that, it thrived. Instead of continuing the business practices of the previous owners, the wicked businessman altered his newly attained factory to the point it no longer resembled its former self.

At first the wicked businessman's customers did not notice a thing, but as time went on, they began to see changes. Unbeknownst to them, the wicked businessman bought not only that factory but also every other factory in the area, and he co-opted them as well. A problem soon arose for the wicked businessman's customers; the wicked businessman monopolized the local economy, leaving them with nothing but faulty products.

This is the explanation of the parable: the wicked businessman represents *Progressives*, the factories represent societal institutions, and the wicked businessman's customers represent unwitting people who rely on those institutions.

Progressives take over sound organizations like political parties, labor unions, charities, and corporations in an attempt to cash in on their good reputations. They do this over and over again because they know highly regarded bodies like churches and schools with good traditions will never be questioned by the public, at least not right away, and that gives them plenty of time to change the landscape before anyone notices. The problem is that if this happens too often, people get left with worthless institutions that are no longer capable of doing any good, and when that happens, there is no where to turn.

Progressives try to nix everything before they try to fix everything.

Evil will enlarge wherever evil is in charge.

Corrupt drivers only drive toward corruption.

Fabianism fabricates *communism*.

Defensive Action

A beast not fed brings no dread.

Marginalized foes never reach the margin.

The fences are defenses.

Bull does not work where there are *bulwarks*.

Thieves will not enter if the door is kept closed.

Holding ground is easier than retaking it.

Small fires need to be extinguished before they become raging infernos.

A little prevention goes a long way in averting a major struggle.

Complacency

A gardener was supposed to prune vines within a patch. This gardener neglected his duty while the vines were small and his work would still be easy.

He thought he could relax, because he believed in his mind the vines could not grow very large. Before the gardener knew it, the vines were huge, and they overshadowed the plants within the patch. After pondering what had happened, the once complacent gardener was bewildered; he had no idea how the vines would be hewed down.

This is the explanation of the parable: the gardener represents voters, the vines represent government, the patch represents the state, and the plants within the patch represent liberty.

Government is growing far beyond its lawful bounds because voters are not removing politicians who are a threat to their liberty. Eventually, these politicians will become entrenched, and removing them will be very hard.

Snares and hares multiply unexpectedly.

Cute little cubs grow to be huge, gnarly bears.

Fall asleep complacent, and you will wake up oppressed.

Heads are in the sand before they are in a noose.

Unattended trouble turns everything to rubble.

A peaceful village knew a violent horde loomed over the horizon. The villagers did nothing while the horde was still far enough away; they just went on with their lives as if nothing could happen.

One day a brave man finally stood up and said, "We had better face reality; if we do nothing, the horde will come upon us, and we will be slaughtered." The village leaders and most of the villagers just scoffed at the man; they put him in prison to shut him up, and they continued as they were.

Eventually, the horde made its way to the village, and it leveled everything. It took away slaves, and as expected, the villagers regretted everything they did.

This is the explanation of the parable: the village and the villagers represent comfortable societies, the horde represents political danger, and the man who stood up to speak out represents unpopular voices.

Political danger always looms, no matter the situation. You cannot ignore threats; you must face them before it is too late. Also, do not dismiss credible people outright; you need to hear what they have to say because they might save your life.

Judgment is in store when it is not stored in our minds.

Occurrences are most likely to occur whenever it is least likely believed they can.

Safety comes when *apathy* goes.

For every inaction there is an equal and opposite undesired reaction.

To not do anything to prevent catastrophe is to do everything to assure it.

Everything is done after nothing is done.

Often it is too late for those who act late.

To those who do nothing for too long, it is just a matter of time before God says so long.

People who kick the can down the road get kicked in the can down the road.

Apathy is the path to tragedy.

Lukewarm societies are puke worn societies.[25]

Flabby souls produce shabby holes.

Duplicity

The unstable are unable.

Schizophrenia creates *schisms*.

Middle Ground

Lack of virtue is not a virtue.

The integrity of the republic is compromised every time the public compromises its principles.

Little philosophical agreement generates much political appeasement.

Lack of cohesion gives rise to stacks of confusions.

Many factions make for fewer actions.

Placation is hell's plantation.

More masters, more disasters

Those who waver savor favor.

Swing voters swing the public from one end of the spectra to the other.

There is no such thing as moderates; a moderate is either a liberal who will not stand to take or a conservative who will not take a stand.

Middle ground is mired ground.

Those who slowly go to the middle quickly go down the drain.

Mediocrity is the cavity which detains pre-eminency.

Anything not headed in the right direction is headed in the wrong direction.

Centrists and *hedonists* are on route to be routed.

If devastation is your destination, take the path with least hesitation.

A death caused by *dearth* goes on for many days without so much as an ounce of *mirth*. [26]

Better to be in a pine box than to pine away.

Final Words

Listen up, O men of war.
The fight is on for the nation's core.
Can you see all the sin?
The urge is strong to just fit in.

We do not fight against flesh and blood.
Though we fight to stop the flood.
The weak back down to save their life.
But we must stand at the sound of strife.

We cannot sit idly by.
Satan wants us all to die.
He may win, and he may lose.
It all depends on what we choose.

Draw your *Sword* and do not look back.
The enemy is poised for his attack.
We can win, that much is sure.
That is—if our hearts are pure.

The world loves its very own.
Just remember we are not alone.
The fight is God's, the One above.
Just serve Him with a lot of love.

Notes

Section A: References

References listed correspond to numbered annotations within the text. All biblical quotes are taken from the King James Version of the Bible.

Chapter I: God

1) "Now therefore, O LORD our God, I beseech thee, save thou us out of his hand, that all the kingdoms of the earth may know that thou art the LORD God, even thou only" (2 Kings 19:19).
2) "Hear, O Israel: The LORD our God is one LORD" (Deuteronomy 6:4).
3) "And God saw every thing that he had made, and, behold, it was very good. And the evening and the morning were the sixth day" (Genesis 1:31).
4) "⁶ They lavish gold out of the bag, and weigh silver in the balance, and hire a goldsmith; and he maketh it a god: they fall down, yea, they worship. ⁷ They bear him upon the shoulder, they carry him, and set him in his place, and he standeth; from his place shall he not remove: yea, one shall cry unto him, yet can he not answer, nor save him out of his trouble" (Isaiah 46:6-7).
5) "God is not a man, that he should lie; neither the son of man, that he should repent: hath he said, and shall he not do it? or hath he spoken, and shall he not make it good" (Numbers 23:19)?
6) "And God said, Let us make man in our image, after our likeness: and let them have dominion over the fish of the sea, and over the fowl of the air, and over the cattle, and over all the earth, and over every creeping thing that creepeth upon the earth." (Genesis 1:26).
7) "God is a Spirit: and they that worship him must worship him in spirit and in truth" (John 4:24).

8) "For there are three that bear record in heaven, the Father, the Word, and the Holy Ghost: and these three are one" (1 John 5:7).
9) "And we have seen and do testify that the Father sent the Son to be the Saviour of the world" (1 John 4:14).
10) "[1] In the beginning was the Word, and the Word was with God, and the Word was God. [2] The same was in the beginning with God. [3] All things were made by him; and without him was not any thing made that was made. [4] In him was life; and the life was the light of men. [5] And the light shineth in darkness; and the darkness comprehended it not. [6] There was a man sent from God, whose name was John. [7] The same came for a witness, to bear witness of the Light, that all men through him might believe. [8] He was not that Light, but was sent to bear witness of that Light. [9] That was the true Light, which lighteth every man that cometh into the world. [10] He was in the world, and the world was made by him, and the world knew him not" (John 1:1-10).
11) "[12] Giving thanks unto the Father, which hath made us meet to be partakers of the inheritance of the saints in light: [13] Who hath delivered us from the power of darkness, and hath translated us into the kingdom of his dear Son: [14] In whom we have redemption through his blood, even the forgiveness of sins: [15] Who is the image of the invisible God, the firstborn of every creature" (Colossians 1:12-15).
12) "Jesus saith unto him, Have I been so long time with you, and yet hast thou not known me, Philip? he that hath seen me hath seen the Father; and how sayest thou then, Shew us the Father" (John 14:9)?
13) "But when the Comforter is come, whom I will send unto you from the Father, even the Spirit of truth, which proceedeth from the Father, he shall testify of me" (John 15:26).
14) "[24] I said, O my God, take me not away in the midst of my days: thy years are throughout all generations. [25] Of old hast thou laid the foundation of the earth: and the heavens are the work of thy hands. [26] They shall perish, but thou shalt endure: yea, all of them shall wax old like a garment; as a vesture shalt thou change them, and they shall be changed: [27] But thou art the same, and thy years shall have no end" (Psalm 102:24-27).

15) "[21] Because that, when they knew God, they glorified him not as God, neither were thankful; but became vain in their imaginations, and their foolish heart was darkened. [22] Professing themselves to be wise, they became fools, [23] And changed the glory of the uncorruptible God into an image made like to corruptible man, and to birds, and four-footed beasts, and creeping things. [24] Wherefore God also gave them up to uncleanness through the lusts of their own hearts, to dishonour their own bodies between themselves: [25] Who changed the truth of God into a lie, and worshipped and served the creature more than the Creator, who is blessed for ever. Amen" (Romans 1:21-25).
16) "[8] The LORD is merciful and gracious, slow to anger, and plenteous in mercy.[9] He will not always chide: neither will he keep his anger for ever" (Psalm 103:8-9).
17) "[12] And to the angel of the church in Pergamos write; These things saith he which hath the sharp sword with two edges; [13] I know thy works, and where thou dwellest, even where Satan's seat is: and thou holdest fast my name, and hast not denied my faith, even in those days wherein Antipas was my faithful martyr, who was slain among you, where Satan dwelleth. [14] But I have a few things against thee, because thou hast there them that hold the doctrine of Balaam, who taught Balac to cast a stumblingblock before the children of Israel, to eat things sacrificed unto idols, and to commit fornication. [15] So hast thou also them that hold the doctrine of the Nicolaitans, which thing I hate. [16] Repent; or else I will come unto thee quickly, and will fight against them with the sword of my mouth." (Revelation 2:12-16),
18) "[5] And one of the elders saith unto me, Weep not: behold, the Lion of the tribe of Juda, the Root of David, hath prevailed to open the book, and to loose the seven seals thereof. [6] And I beheld, and, lo, in the midst of the throne and of the four beasts, and in the midst of the elders, stood a Lamb as it had been slain, having seven horns and seven eyes, which are the seven Spirits of God sent forth into all the earth. [7] And he came and took the book out of the right hand of him that sat upon the throne. [8] And when he had taken the book, the four beasts and four and twenty elders fell down before the Lamb, having every one of them harps, and golden vials full of odours, which are the prayers of saints. [9] And they sung a new song, saying, Thou art worthy to take

the book, and to open the seals thereof: for thou wast slain, and hast redeemed us to God by thy blood out of every kindred, and tongue, and people, and nation; [10] And hast made us unto our God kings and priests: and we shall reign on the earth" (Revelation 5:5-10).

19) "It is the glory of God to conceal a thing: but the honour of kings is to search out a matter" (Proverbs 25:2).

20) "[17] And the LORD said unto Moses, I will do this thing also that thou hast spoken: for thou hast found grace in my sight, and I know thee by name. [18] And he said, I beseech thee, shew me thy glory. [19] And he said, I will make all my goodness pass before thee, and I will proclaim the name of the LORD before thee; and will be gracious to whom I will be gracious, and will shew mercy on whom I will shew mercy. [20] And he said, Thou canst not see my face: for there shall no man see me, and live" (Exodus 33:17-20).

21) "The heavens declare the glory of God; and the firmament sheweth his handywork" (Psalm 19:1)

22) "[15] The LORD thy God will raise up unto thee a Prophet from the midst of thee, of thy brethren, like unto me; unto him ye shall hearken; [16] According to all that thou desiredst of the LORD thy God in Horeb in the day of the assembly, saying, Let me not hear again the voice of the LORD my God, neither let me see this great fire any more, that I die not. [17] And the LORD said unto me, They have well spoken that which they have spoken. [18] I will raise them up a Prophet from among their brethren, like unto thee, and will put my words in his mouth; and he shall speak unto them all that I shall command him. [19] And it shall come to pass, that whosoever will not hearken unto my words which he shall speak in my name, I will require it of him" (Deuteronomy 18:15-19).

23) "[18] And all things are of God, who hath reconciled us to himself by Jesus Christ, and hath given to us the ministry of reconciliation; [19] To wit, that God was in Christ, reconciling the world unto himself, not imputing their trespasses unto them; and hath committed unto us the word of reconciliation. [20] Now then we are ambassadors for Christ, as though God did beseech you by us: we pray you in Christ's stead, be ye reconciled to God. [21] For he hath made him to be sin

for us, who knew no sin; that we might be made the righteousness of God in him" (2 Corinthians 5:18-21).

24) "[9] "But we see Jesus, who was made a little lower than the angels for the suffering of death, crowned with glory and honour; that he by the grace of God should taste death for every man. [10] For it became him, for whom are all things, and by whom are all things, in bringing many sons unto glory, to make the captain of their salvation perfect through sufferings" (Hebrews 2:9-10).

25) "[18] Forasmuch as ye know that ye were not redeemed with corruptible things, as silver and gold, from your vain conversation received by tradition from your fathers; [19] But with the precious blood of Christ, as of a lamb without blemish and without spot" (1 Peter 1:18-19).

26) "[25] Then he said unto them, O fools, and slow of heart to believe all that the prophets have spoken: [26] Ought not Christ to have suffered these things, and to enter into his glory? [27] And beginning at Moses and all the prophets, he expounded unto them in all the scriptures the things concerning himself" (Luke 24:25-27).

27) "For even the Son of man came not to be ministered unto, but to minister, and to give his life a ransom for many" (Mark 10:45).

28) "[48] I am that bread of life. [49] Your fathers did eat manna in the wilderness, and are dead. [50] This is the bread which cometh down from heaven, that a man may eat thereof, and not die. [51] I am the living bread which came down from heaven: if any man eat of this bread, he shall live for ever: and the bread that I will give is my flesh, which I will give for the life of the world. [52] The Jews therefore strove among themselves, saying, How can this man give us his flesh to eat? [53] Then Jesus said unto them, Verily, verily, I say unto you, Except ye eat the flesh of the Son of man, and drink his blood, ye have no life in you. [54] Whoso eateth my flesh, and drinketh my blood, hath eternal life; and I will raise him up at the last day. [55] For my flesh is meat indeed, and my blood is drink indeed. [56] He that eateth my flesh, and drinketh my blood, dwelleth in me, and I in him. [57] As the living Father hath sent me, and I live by the Father: so he that eateth me, even he shall live by me. [58] This is that bread which came down from heaven: not as your fathers did eat manna, and are dead: he that eateth of this bread shall live for ever" (John 6:48-58).

29) "[14] Ye are my friends, if ye do whatsoever I command you. [15] Henceforth I call you not servants; for the servant knoweth not what his lord doeth: but I have called you friends; for all things that I have heard of my Father I have made known unto you. [16] Ye have not chosen me, but I have chosen you, and ordained you, that ye should go and bring forth fruit, and that your fruit should remain: that whatsoever ye shall ask of the Father in my name, he may give it you" (John 15:14-16).

30) "[26] For if we sin wilfully after that we have received the knowledge of the truth, there remaineth no more sacrifice for sins, [27] But a certain fearful looking for of judgment and fiery indignation, which shall devour the adversaries. [28] He that despised Moses' law died without mercy under two or three witnesses: [29] Of how much sorer punishment, suppose ye, shall he be thought worthy, who hath trodden under foot the Son of God, and hath counted the blood of the covenant, wherewith he was sanctified, an unholy thing, and hath done despite unto the Spirit of grace" (Hebrews 10:26-29)?

31) "[10] Therefore fear thou not, O my servant Jacob, saith the LORD; neither be dismayed, O Israel: for, lo, I will save thee from afar, and thy seed from the land of their captivity; and Jacob shall return, and shall be in rest, and be quiet, and none shall make him afraid. [11] For I am with thee, saith the LORD, to save thee: though I make a full end of all nations whither I have scattered thee, yet will I not make a full end of thee: but I will correct thee in measure, and will not leave thee altogether unpunished" (Jeremiah 30:10-11).

32) "[1] I say then, Hath God cast away his people? God forbid. For I also am an Israelite, of the seed of Abraham, of the tribe of Benjamin. [2] God hath not cast away his people which he foreknew. Wot ye not what the scripture saith of Elias? how he maketh intercession to God against Israel, saying, [3] Lord, they have killed thy prophets, and digged down thine altars; and I am left alone, and they seek my life. [4] But what saith the answer of God unto him? I have reserved to myself seven thousand men, who have not bowed the knee to the image of Baal. [5] Even so then at this present time also there is a remnant according to the election of grace" (Romans 11:1-5).

33) "That the Gentiles should be fellowheirs, and of the same body, and partakers of his promise in Christ by the gospel" (Ephesians 3:6).

34) "[38] And John answered him, saying, Master, we saw one casting out devils in thy name, and he followeth not us: and we forbad him, because he followeth not us. [39] But Jesus said, Forbid him not: for there is no man which shall do a miracle in my name, that can lightly speak evil of me. [40] For he that is not against us is on our part. [41] For whosoever shall give you a cup of water to drink in my name, because ye belong to Christ, verily I say unto you, he shall not lose his reward" (Mark 9:38-41).

35) "[24] God that made the world and all things therein, seeing that he is Lord of heaven and earth, dwelleth not in temples made with hands; [25] Neither is worshipped with men's hands, as though he needed any thing, seeing he giveth to all life, and breath, and all things; [26] And hath made of one blood all nations of men for to dwell on all the face of the earth, and hath determined the times before appointed, and the bounds of their habitation" (Acts 17:24-26).

36) "[7] What then? Israel hath not obtained that which he seeketh for; but the election hath obtained it, and the rest were blinded [8] (According as it is written, God hath given them the spirit of slumber, eyes that they should not see, and ears that they should not hear;) unto this day. [9] And David saith, Let their table be made a snare, and a trap, and a stumbling block, and a recompence unto them: [10] Let their eyes be darkened, that they may not see, and bow down their back alway. [11] I say then, Have they stumbled that they should fall? God forbid: but rather through their fall salvation is come unto the Gentiles, for to provoke them to jealousy. [12] Now if the fall of them be the riches of the world, and the diminishing of them the riches of the Gentiles; how much more their fulness? [13] For I speak to you Gentiles, inasmuch as I am the apostle of the Gentiles, I magnify mine office: [14] If by any means I may provoke to emulation them which are my flesh, and might save some of them. [15] For if the casting away of them be the reconciling of the world, what shall the receiving of them be, but life from the dead? [16] For if the firstfruit be holy, the lump is also holy: and if the root be holy, so are the branches. [17] And if some of the branches be broken off, and thou, being a wild olive tree, wert graffed in among them, and with them partakest of the root and fatness of the olive tree" (Romans 11:7-17).

37) "[1] Now the LORD had said unto Abram, Get thee out of thy country, and from thy kindred, and from thy father's house, unto a land that I will shew thee: [2] And I will make of thee a great nation, and I will bless thee, and make thy name great; and thou shalt be a blessing; [3] And I will bless them that bless thee, and curse him that curseth thee: and in thee shall all families of the earth be blessed" (Genesis 12:1-3).

38) "But thou, Bethlehem Ephratah, though thou be little among the thousands of Judah, yet out of thee shall he come forth unto me that is to be ruler in Israel; whose goings forth have been from of old, from everlasting" (Micah 5:2).

39) "Thou art worthy, O Lord, to receive glory and honour and power: for thou hast created all things, and for thy pleasure they are and were created" (Revelation 4:11).

40) "Lo, this only have I found, that God hath made man upright; but they have sought out many inventions" (Ecclesiastes 7:29).

41) "Behold, the LORD's hand is not shortened, that it cannot save; neither his ear heavy, that it cannot hear" (Isaiah 59:1).

42) "[11] Thine, O LORD, is the greatness, and the power, and the glory, and the victory, and the majesty: for all that is in the heaven and in the earth is thine; thine is the kingdom, O LORD, and thou art exalted as head above all. [12] Both riches and honour come of thee, and thou reignest over all; and in thine hand is power and might; and in thine hand it is to make great, and to give strength unto all" (1 Chronicles 29:11-12).

43) "[20] And when he was demanded of the Pharisees, when the kingdom of God should come, he answered them and said, The kingdom of God cometh not with observation: [21] Neither shall they say, Lo here! or, lo there! for, behold, the kingdom of God is within you" (Luke 17:20-21).

44) "[23] And it came to pass in process of time, that the king of Egypt died: and the children of Israel sighed by reason of the bondage, and they cried, and their cry came up unto God by reason of the bondage. [24] And God heard their groaning, and God remembered his covenant with Abraham, with Isaac, and with Jacob. [25] And God looked upon the children of Israel, and God had respect unto them" (Exodus 2:23-25).

45) "He shall pray unto God, and he will be favourable unto him: and he shall see his face with joy: for he will render unto man his righteousness" (Job 33:26).
46) "[13] And whatsoever ye shall ask in my name, that will I do, that the Father may be glorified in the Son. [14] If ye shall ask any thing in my name, I will do it" (John 14:13-14).
47) "[43] Jesus therefore answered and said unto them, Murmur not among yourselves. [44] No man can come to me, except the Father which hath sent me draw him: and I will raise him up at the last day" (John 6:43-44).
48) "[28] And we know that all things work together for good to them that love God, to them who are the called according to his purpose. [29] For whom he did foreknow, he also did predestinate to be conformed to the image of his Son, that he might be the firstborn among many brethren. [30] Moreover whom he did predestinate, them he also called: and whom he called, them he also justified: and whom he justified, them he also glorified. [31] What shall we then say to these things? If God be for us, who can be against us?" (Romans 8:28-31).
49) "Wherefore the law was our schoolmaster to bring us unto Christ, that we might be justified by faith" (Galatians 3:24).
50) "[12] And now, Israel, what doth the LORD thy God require of thee, but to fear the LORD thy God, to walk in all his ways, and to love him, and to serve the LORD thy God with all thy heart and with all thy soul, [13] To keep the commandments of the LORD, and his statutes, which I command thee this day for thy good" (Deuteronomy 10:12-13)?
51) "[6] For promotion cometh neither from the east, nor from the west, nor from the south. [7] But God is the judge: he putteth down one, and setteth up another" (Psalm 75:6-7).
52) "[6] Wherein ye greatly rejoice, though now for a season, if need be, ye are in heaviness through manifold temptations: [7] That the trial of your faith, being much more precious than of gold that perisheth, though it be tried with fire, might be found unto praise and honour and glory at the appearing of Jesus Christ: [8] Whom having not seen, ye love; in whom, though now ye see him not, yet believing, ye rejoice with joy unspeakable and full of glory: [9] Receiving the end of your faith, even the salvation of your souls" (1 Peter 1:6-9).

53) "There hath no temptation taken you but such as is common to man: but God is faithful, who will not suffer you to be tempted above that ye are able; but will with the temptation also make a way to escape, that ye may be able to bear it" (1 Corinthians 10:13).
54) "[43] Jesus therefore answered and said unto them, Murmur not among yourselves. [44] No man can come to me, except the Father which hath sent me draw him: and I will raise him up at the last day" (John 6:43-44).
55) "Whosoever shall seek to save his life shall lose it; and whosoever shall lose his life shall preserve it" (Luke 17:33).
56) "And the LORD was with Jehoshaphat, because he walked in the first ways of his father David, and sought not unto Baalim" (2 Chronicles 17:3).

Chapter 2: Morality & The Human Condition

1) "[38] And he that taketh not his cross, and followeth after me, is not worthy of me. [39] He that findeth his life shall lose it: and he that loseth his life for my sake shall find it" (Matthew 10:38-39).
2) "[14] What doth it profit, my brethren, though a man say he hath faith, and have not works? can faith save him? [15] If a brother or sister be naked, and destitute of daily food, [16] And one of you say unto them, Depart in peace, be ye warmed and filled; notwithstanding ye give them not those things which are needful to the body; what doth it profit? [17] Even so faith, if it hath not works, is dead, being alone. [18] Yea, a man may say, Thou hast faith, and I have works: shew me thy faith without thy works, and I will shew thee my faith by my works. [19] Thou believest that there is one God; thou doest well: the devils also believe, and tremble. [20] But wilt thou know, O vain man, that faith without works is dead? [21] Was not Abraham our father justified by works, when he had offered Isaac his son upon the altar? [22] Seest thou how faith wrought with his works, and by works was faith made perfect? [23] And the scripture was fulfilled which saith, Abraham believed God, and it was imputed unto him for righteousness: and he was called the Friend of God. [24] Ye see then how that by works a man is justi-

fied, and not by faith only. [25] Likewise also was not Rahab the harlot justified by works, when she had received the messengers, and had sent them out another way? [26] For as the body without the spirit is dead, so faith without works is dead also" (James 2:14-26).

3) "[1] Therefore being justified by faith, we have peace with God through our Lord Jesus Christ: [2] By whom also we have access by faith into this grace wherein we stand, and rejoice in hope of the glory of God" (Romans 5:1-2).

4) "No man can serve two masters: for either he will hate the one, and love the other; or else he will hold to the one, and despise the other. Ye cannot serve God and mammon" (Matthew 6:24).

5) "And whosoever shall exalt himself shall be abased; and he that shall humble himself shall be exalted" (Matthew 23:12).

6) "[6] And ye became followers of us, and of the Lord, having received the word in much affliction, with joy of the Holy Ghost: [7] So that ye were ensamples to all that believe in Macedonia and Achaia" (1 Thessalonians 1:6-7).

7) "[13] And David said unto Nathan, I have sinned against the LORD. And Nathan said unto David, The LORD also hath put away thy sin; thou shalt not die. [14] Howbeit, because by this deed thou hast given great occasion to the enemies of the LORD to blaspheme, the child also that is born unto thee shall surely die" (2 Samuel 12:13-14).

8) "Ye are the salt of the earth: but if the salt have lost his savour, wherewith shall it be salted? it is thenceforth good for nothing, but to be cast out, and to be trodden under foot of men" (Matthew 5:13).

9) "As a dog returneth to his vomit, so a fool returneth to his folly" (Proverbs 26:11).

10) "Blessed are ye that hunger now: for ye shall be filled. Blessed are ye that weep now: for ye shall laugh" (Luke 6:21).

11) "[9] And Jesus said unto him, This day is salvation come to this house, forsomuch as he also is a son of Abraham. [10] For the Son of man is come to seek and to save that which was lost" (Luke 19:9-10).

12) "The wicked, through the pride of his countenance, will not seek after God: God is not in all his thoughts" (Psalm 10:4).

13) "A man's pride shall bring him low: but honour shall uphold the humble in spirit" (Proverbs 29:23).

14) "Then when lust hath conceived, it bringeth forth sin: and sin, when it is finished, bringeth forth death" (James 1:15).
15) "Let us hear the conclusion of the whole matter: Fear God, and keep his commandments: for this is the whole duty of man" (Ecclesiastes 12:13).
16) "And let us not be weary in well doing: for in due season we shall reap, if we faint not" (Galatians 6:9).
17) " [21] I find then a law, that, when I would do good, evil is present with me. [22] For I delight in the law of God after the inward man: [23] But I see another law in my members, warring against the law of my mind, and bringing me into captivity to the law of sin which is in my members" (Romans 7:21-23).
18) "[10] And the disciples came, and said unto him, Why speakest thou unto them in parables? [11] He answered and said unto them, Because it is given unto you to know the mysteries of the kingdom of heaven, but to them it is not given. [12] For whosoever hath, to him shall be given, and he shall have more abundance: but whosoever hath not, from him shall be taken away even that he hath. [13] Therefore speak I to them in parables: because they seeing see not; and hearing they hear not, neither do they understand. [14] And in them is fulfilled the prophecy of Esaias, which saith, By hearing ye shall hear, and shall not understand; and seeing ye shall see, and shall not perceive: [15] For this people's heart is waxed gross, and their ears are dull of hearing, and their eyes they have closed; lest at any time they should see with their eyes, and hear with their ears, and should understand with their heart, and should be converted, and I should heal them. [16] But blessed are your eyes, for they see: and your ears, for they hear. [17] For verily I say unto you, That many prophets and righteous men have desired to see those things which ye see, and have not seen them; and to hear those things which ye hear, and have not heard them" (Matthew 13:10-17).
19) "[1] And God spake all these words, saying, [2] I am the LORD thy God, which have brought thee out of the land of Egypt, out of the house of bondage. [3] Thou shalt have no other gods before me. [4] Thou shalt not make unto thee any graven image, or any likeness of any thing that is in heaven above, or that is in the earth beneath, or that is in

the water under the earth: [5] Thou shalt not bow down thyself to them, nor serve them: for I the LORD thy God am a jealous God, visiting the iniquity of the fathers upon the children unto the third and fourth generation of them that hate me; [6] And shewing mercy unto thousands of them that love me, and keep my commandments. [7] Thou shalt not take the name of the LORD thy God in vain; for the LORD will not hold him guiltless that taketh his name in vain. [8] Remember the sabbath day, to keep it holy. [9] Six days shalt thou labour, and do all thy work: [10] But the seventh day is the sabbath of the LORD thy God: in it thou shalt not do any work, thou, nor thy son, nor thy daughter, thy manservant, nor thy maidservant, nor thy cattle, nor thy stranger that is within thy gates: [11] For in six days the LORD made heaven and earth, the sea, and all that in them is, and rested the seventh day: wherefore the LORD blessed the sabbath day, and hallowed it. [12] Honour thy father and thy mother: that thy days may be long upon the land which the LORD thy God giveth thee. [13] Thou shalt not kill. [14] Thou shalt not commit adultery. [15] Thou shalt not steal. [16] Thou shalt not bear false witness against thy neighbour. [17] Thou shalt not covet thy neighbour's house, thou shalt not covet thy neighbour's wife, nor his manservant, nor his maidservant, nor his ox, nor his ass, nor any thing that is thy neighbour's" (Exodus 20:1-17).

20) "[35] Then one of them, which was a lawyer, asked him a question, tempting him, and saying, [36] Master, which is the great commandment in the law? [37] Jesus said unto him, Thou shalt love the Lord thy God with all thy heart, and with all thy soul, and with all thy mind. [38] This is the first and great commandment. [39] And the second is like unto it, Thou shalt love thy neighbour as thyself. [40] On these two commandments hang all the law and the prophets" (Matthew 22:35-40).

21) "But he that received seed into the good ground is he that heareth the word, and understandeth it; which also beareth fruit, and bringeth forth, some an hundredfold, some sixty, some thirty" (Matthew 13:23).

22) "[19] When any one heareth the word of the kingdom, and understandeth it not, then cometh the wicked one, and catcheth away that which was sown in his heart. This is he which received seed by the way side. [20] But he that received the seed into stony places, the same is he that

heareth the word, and anon with joy receiveth it; [21] Yet hath he not root in himself, but dureth for a while: for when tribulation or persecution ariseth because of the word, by and by he is offended. [22] He also that received seed among the thorns is he that heareth the word; and the care of this world, and the deceitfulness of riches, choke the word, and he becometh unfruitful" (Matthew 13:19-22).

23) "[17] Think not that I am come to destroy the law, or the prophets: I am not come to destroy, but to fulfil. [18] For verily I say unto you, Till heaven and earth pass, one jot or one tittle shall in no wise pass from the law, till all be fulfilled" (Matthew 5:17-18).

24) "[37] And the Father himself, which hath sent me, hath borne witness of me. Ye have neither heard his voice at any time, nor seen his shape. [38] And ye have not his word abiding in you: for whom he hath sent, him ye believe not. [39] Search the scriptures; for in them ye think ye have eternal life: and they are they which testify of me" (John 5:37-39).

25) "[10] If thou shalt hearken unto the voice of the LORD thy God, to keep his commandments and his statutes which are written in this book of the law, and if thou turn unto the LORD thy God with all thine heart, and with all thy soul. [11] For this commandment which I command thee this day, it is not hidden from thee, neither is it far off. [12] It is not in heaven, that thou shouldest say, Who shall go up for us to heaven, and bring it unto us, that we may hear it, and do it? [13] Neither is it beyond the sea, that thou shouldest say, Who shall go over the sea for us, and bring it unto us, that we may hear it, and do it? [14] But the word is very nigh unto thee, in thy mouth, and in thy heart, that thou mayest do it" (Deuteronomy 30:10-14).

26) "[19] And this is the condemnation, that light is come into the world, and men loved darkness rather than light, because their deeds were evil. [20] For every one that doeth evil hateth the light, neither cometh to the light, lest his deeds should be reproved" (John 3:19-20).

27) "[16] All scripture is given by inspiration of God, and is profitable for doctrine, for reproof, for correction, for instruction in righteousness: [17] That the man of God may be perfect, throughly furnished unto all good works" (2 Timothy 3:16-17).

28) "The fear of the LORD is the beginning of knowledge: but fools despise wisdom and instruction" (Proverbs 1:7).

29) "What shall we then say to these things? If God be for us, who can be against us" (Romans 8:31).
30) "[39] And Jesus said, For judgment I am come into this world, that they which see not might see; and that they which see might be made blind. [40] And some of the Pharisees which were with him heard these words, and said unto him, Are we blind also? [41] Jesus said unto them, If ye were blind, ye should have no sin: but now ye say, We see; therefore your sin remaineth" (John 9:39-41).
31) "[12] For as many as have sinned without law shall also perish without law: and as many as have sinned in the law shall be judged by the law; [13] (For not the hearers of the law are just before God, but the doers of the law shall be justified. [14] For when the Gentiles, which have not the law, do by nature the things contained in the law, these, having not the law, are a law unto themselves: [15] Which shew the work of the law written in their hearts, their conscience also bearing witness, and their thoughts the mean while accusing or else excusing one another;) [16] In the day when God shall judge the secrets of men by Jesus Christ according to my gospel" (Romans 2:12-16).
32) "[20] But ye have not so learned Christ; [21] If so be that ye have heard him, and have been taught by him, as the truth is in Jesus: [22] That ye put off concerning the former conversation the old man, which is corrupt according to the deceitful lusts; [23] And be renewed in the spirit of your mind; [24] And that ye put on the new man, which after God is created in righteousness and true holiness" (Ephesians 4:20-24).
33) "And the Spirit of the LORD will come upon thee, and thou shalt prophesy with them, and shalt be turned into another man" (1 Samuel 10:6).
34) "[3] Jesus answered and said unto him, Verily, verily, I say unto thee, Except a man be born again, he cannot see the kingdom of God. [4] Nicodemus saith unto him, How can a man be born when he is old? can he enter the second time into his mother's womb, and be born? [5] Jesus answered, Verily, verily, I say unto thee, Except a man be born of water and of the Spirit, he cannot enter into the kingdom of God. [6] That which is born of the flesh is flesh; and that which is born of the Spirit is spirit. [7] Marvel not that I said unto thee, Ye must be born again. [8] The wind bloweth where it listeth, and thou hearest the sound

thereof, but canst not tell whence it cometh, and whither it goeth: so is every one that is born of the Spirit" (John 3:3-8).

35) "[13] Enter ye in at the strait gate: for wide is the gate, and broad is the way, that leadeth to destruction, and many there be which go in thereat: [14] Because strait is the gate, and narrow is the way, which leadeth unto life, and few there be that find it" (Matthew 7:13-14).

36) "[21] Art thou called being a servant? care not for it: but if thou mayest be made free, use it rather. [22] For he that is called in the Lord, being a servant, is the Lord's freeman: likewise also he that is called, being free, is Christ's servant. [23] Ye are bought with a price; be not ye the servants of men" (1 Corinthians 7:21-23).

37) "[15] Beware of false prophets, which come to you in sheep's clothing, but inwardly they are ravening wolves. [16] Ye shall know them by their fruits. Do men gather grapes of thorns, or figs of thistles? [17] Even so every good tree bringeth forth good fruit; but a corrupt tree bringeth forth evil fruit. [18] A good tree cannot bring forth evil fruit, neither can a corrupt tree bring forth good fruit. [19] Every tree that bringeth not forth good fruit is hewn down, and cast into the fire. [20] Wherefore by their fruits ye shall know them" (Matthew 7:15-20).

38) "[1] At the same time came the disciples unto Jesus, saying, Who is the greatest in the kingdom of heaven? [2] And Jesus called a little child unto him, and set him in the midst of them, [3] And said, Verily I say unto you, Except ye be converted, and become as little children, ye shall not enter into the kingdom of heaven. [4] Whosoever therefore shall humble himself as this little child, the same is greatest in the kingdom of heaven" (Matthew 18:1-4).

39) "And he sat down, and called the twelve, and saith unto them, If any man desire to be first, the same shall be last of all, and servant of all" (Mark 9:35).

40) "[2] Hereby know ye the Spirit of God: Every spirit that confesseth that Jesus Christ is come in the flesh is of God: [3] And every spirit that confesseth not that Jesus Christ is come in the flesh is not of God: and this is that spirit of antichrist, whereof ye have heard that it should come; and even now already is it in the world. [4] Ye are of God, little children, and have overcome them: because greater is he that is in you, than he that is in the world" (1 John 4:2-4).

41) "[15] See, I have set before thee this day life and good, and death and evil; [16] In that I command thee this day to love the LORD thy God, to walk in his ways, and to keep his commandments and his statutes and his judgments, that thou mayest live and multiply: and the LORD thy God shall bless thee in the land whither thou goest to possess it. [17] But if thine heart turn away, so that thou wilt not hear, but shalt be drawn away, and worship other gods, and serve them; [18] I denounce unto you this day, that ye shall surely perish, and that ye shall not prolong your days upon the land, whither thou passest over Jordan to go to possess it. [19] I call heaven and earth to record this day against you, that I have set before you life and death, blessing and cursing: therefore choose life, that both thou and thy seed may live: [20] That thou mayest love the LORD thy God, and that thou mayest obey his voice, and that thou mayest cleave unto him: for he is thy life, and the length of thy days: that thou mayest dwell in the land which the LORD sware unto thy fathers, to Abraham, to Isaac, and to Jacob, to give them" (Deuteronomy 30:15-20).

42) "[10] Therefore I endure all things for the elect's sakes, that they may also obtain the salvation which is in Christ Jesus with eternal glory. [11] It is a faithful saying: For if we be dead with him, we shall also live with him" (2 Timothy 2:10-11).

Chapter 3: Relationships & Conflict

1) "Fight the good fight of faith, lay hold on eternal life, whereunto thou art also called, and hast professed a good profession before many witnesses" (1 Timothy 6:12).

2) "[6] Although affliction cometh not forth of the dust, neither doth trouble spring out of the ground; [7] Yet man is born unto trouble, as the sparks fly upward" (Job 5:6-7).

3) "[24] Know ye not that they which run in a race run all, but one receiveth the prize? So run, that ye may obtain. [25] And every man that striveth for the mastery is temperate in all things. Now they do it to obtain a corruptible crown; but we an incorruptible" (1 Corinthians 9:24-25).

4) "³ Let the husband render unto the wife due benevolence: and likewise also the wife unto the husband. ⁴ The wife hath not power of her own body, but the husband: and likewise also the husband hath not power of his own body, but the wife" (1 Corinthians 7:3-4).
5) "So God created man in his own image, in the image of God created he him; male and female created he them" (Genesis 1:27).
6) "⁹ What then? are we better than they? No, in no wise: for we have before proved both Jews and Gentiles, that they are all under sin; ¹⁰ As it is written, There is none righteous, no, not one: ¹¹ There is none that understandeth, there is none that seeketh after God. ¹² They are all gone out of the way, they are together become unprofitable; there is none that doeth good, no, not one" (Romans 3:9-12).
7) " ²⁰ But the wicked are like the troubled sea, when it cannot rest, whose waters cast up mire and dirt. ²¹ There is no peace, saith my God, to the wicked" (Isaiah 57:20-21).
8) " ²¹ If thine enemy be hungry, give him bread to eat; and if he be thirsty, give him water to drink: ²² For thou shalt heap coals of fire upon his head, and the LORD shall reward thee" (Proverbs 25:21-22).
9) "Blessed are the merciful: for they shall obtain mercy" (Matthew 5:7).
10) "²⁹ And if thy right eye offend thee, pluck it out, and cast it from thee: for it is profitable for thee that one of thy members should perish, and not that thy whole body should be cast into hell. ³⁰ And if thy right hand offend thee, cut if off, and cast it from thee: for it is profitable for thee that one of thy members should perish, and not that thy whole body should be cast into hell" (Matthew 5:29-30).
11) ³¹ For if we would judge ourselves, we should not be judged. ³² But when we are judged, we are chastened of the Lord, that we should not be condemned with the world" (1 Corinthians 11:31-32).
12) "²⁷ Then answered Peter and said unto him, Behold, we have forsaken all, and followed thee; what shall we have therefore? ²⁸ And Jesus said unto them, Verily I say unto you, That ye which have followed me, in the regeneration when the Son of man shall sit in the throne of his glory, ye also shall sit upon twelve thrones, judging the twelve tribes of Israel. ²⁹ And every one that hath forsaken houses, or brethren, or sisters, or father, or mother, or wife, or children, or lands, for my name's sake, shall receive an hundredfold, and shall inherit everlasting

life. [30] But many that are first shall be last; and the last shall be first" (Matthew 19:27-30).

13) "There is a way which seemeth right unto a man, but the end thereof are the ways of death" (Proverbs 14:12).

14) " [6] And the LORD passed by before him, and proclaimed, The LORD, The LORD God, merciful and gracious, longsuffering, and abundant in goodness and truth, [7] Keeping mercy for thousands, forgiving iniquity and transgression and sin, and that will by no means clear the guilty; visiting the iniquity of the fathers upon the children, and upon the children's children, unto the third and to the fourth generation" (Exodus 34:6-7).

15) "My people are destroyed for lack of knowledge: because thou hast rejected knowledge, I will also reject thee, that thou shalt be no priest to me: seeing thou hast forgotten the law of thy God, I will also forget thy children" (Hosea 4:6).

16) "The rod and reproof give wisdom: but a child left to himself bringeth his mother to shame" (Proverbs 29:15).

17) "Withhold not correction from the child: for if thou beatest him with the rod, he shall not die" (Proverbs 23:13).

18) "Train up a child in the way he should go: and when he is old, he will not depart from it" (Proverbs 22:6).

19) " [41] And Moses said, Wherefore now do ye transgress the commandment of the LORD? but it shall not prosper. [42] Go not up, for the LORD is not among you; that ye be not smitten before your enemies. [43] For the Amalekites and the Canaanites are there before you, and ye shall fall by the sword: because ye are turned away from the LORD, therefore the LORD will not be with you. [44] But they presumed to go up unto the hill top: nevertheless the ark of the covenant of the LORD, and Moses, departed not out of the camp. [45] Then the Amalekites came down, and the Canaanites which dwelt in that hill, and smote them, and discomfited them, even unto Hormah" (Numbers 14:41-45).

20) "Cast out the scorner, and contention shall go out; yea, strife and reproach shall cease" (Proverbs 22:10).

21) "Hatred stirreth up strifes: but love covereth all sins" (Proverbs 10:12).

22) "Prepare thy work without, and make it fit for thyself in the field; and afterwards build thine house" (Proverbs 24:27).

23) "Think not that I am come to send peace on earth: I came not to send peace, but a sword" (Matthew 10:34).

24) "But he, knowing their thoughts, said unto them, Every kingdom divided against itself is brought to desolation; and a house divided against a house falleth" (Luke 11:17).

25) "Man that is in honour, and understandeth not, is like the beasts that perish" (Psalm 49:20).

26) "[1] Again the word of the LORD came unto me, saying, [2] Son of man, speak to the children of thy people, and say unto them, When I bring the sword upon a land, if the people of the land take a man of their coasts, and set him for their watchman: [3] If when he seeth the sword come upon the land, he blow the trumpet, and warn the people; [4] Then whosoever heareth the sound of the trumpet, and taketh not warning; if the sword come, and take him away, his blood shall be upon his own head. [5] He heard the sound of the trumpet, and took not warning; his blood shall be upon him. But he that taketh warning shall deliver his soul. [6] But if the watchman see the sword come, and blow not the trumpet, and the people be not warned; if the sword come, and take any person from among them, he is taken away in his iniquity; but his blood will I require at the watchman's hand" (Ezekiel 33:1-6).

27) "[16] And it came to pass at the end of seven days, that the word of the LORD came unto me, saying, [17] Son of man, I have made thee a watchman unto the house of Israel: therefore hear the word at my mouth, and give them warning from me. [18] When I say unto the wicked, Thou shalt surely die; and thou givest him not warning, nor speakest to warn the wicked from his wicked way, to save his life; the same wicked man shall die in his iniquity; but his blood will I require at thine hand" (Ezekiel 3:16-18).

28) "[15] And the prayer of faith shall save the sick, and the Lord shall raise him up; and if he have committed sins, they shall be forgiven him. [16] Confess your faults one to another, and pray one for another, that ye may be healed. The effectual fervent prayer of a righteous man availeth much" (James 5:15-16).

29) "Correction is grievous unto him that forsaketh the way: and he that hateth reproof shall die" (Proverbs 15:10).

30) "Ye adulterers and adulteresses, know ye not that the friendship of the world is enmity with God? whosoever therefore will be a friend of the world is the enemy of God" (James 4:4).

31) "[25] And there went great multitudes with him: and he turned, and said unto them, [26] If any man come to me, and hate not his father, and mother, and wife, and children, and brethren, and sisters, yea, and his own life also, he cannot be my disciple. [27] And whosoever doth not bear his cross, and come after me, cannot be my disciple. [28] For which of you, intending to build a tower, sitteth not down first, and counteth the cost, whether he have sufficient to finish it? [29] Lest haply, after he hath laid the foundation, and is not able to finish it, all that behold it begin to mock him, [30] Saying, This man began to build, and was not able to finish. [31] Or what king, going to make war against another king, sitteth not down first, and consulteth whether he be able with ten thousand to meet him that cometh against him with twenty thousand? [32] Or else, while the other is yet a great way off, he sendeth an ambassage, and desireth conditions of peace. [33] So likewise, whosoever he be of you that forsaketh not all that he hath, he cannot be my disciple" (Luke 14:25-33).

32) "[18] Let no man deceive himself. If any man among you seemeth to be wise in this world, let him become a fool, that he may be wise. [19] For the wisdom of this world is foolishness with God. For it is written, He taketh the wise in their own craftiness. [20] And again, The Lord knoweth the thoughts of the wise, that they are vain" (1 Corinthians 3:18-20).

33) "[9] For I think that God hath set forth us the apostles last, as it were appointed to death: for we are made a spectacle unto the world, and to angels, and to men. [10] We are fools for Christ's sake, but ye are wise in Christ; we are weak, but ye are strong; ye are honourable, but we are despised. [11] Even unto this present hour we both hunger, and thirst, and are naked, and are buffeted, and have no certain dwellingplace; [12] And labour, working with our own hands: being reviled, we bless; being persecuted, we suffer it: [13] Being defamed, we intreat: we are made as the filth of the world, and are the offscouring of all things unto this day" (1 Corinthians 4:9-13).

34) "¹⁶ Ye have not chosen me, but I have chosen you, and ordained you, that ye should go and bring forth fruit, and that your fruit should remain: that whatsoever ye shall ask of the Father in my name, he may give it you. ¹⁷ These things I command you, that ye love one another. ¹⁸ If the world hate you, ye know that it hated me before it hated you. ¹⁹ If ye were of the world, the world would love his own: but because ye are not of the world, but I have chosen you out of the world, therefore the world hateth you" (John 15:16-19).

35) "¹⁰ Blessed are they which are persecuted for righteousness' sake: for theirs is the kingdom of heaven. ¹¹ Blessed are ye, when men shall revile you, and persecute you, and shall say all manner of evil against you falsely, for my sake. ¹² Rejoice, and be exceeding glad: for great is your reward in heaven: for so persecuted they the prophets which were before you" (Matthew 5:10-12).

36) "Then said Jesus unto him, Put up again thy sword into his place: for all they that take the sword shall perish with the sword" (Matthew 26:52).

37) " ²⁶ And he said, So is the kingdom of God, as if a man should cast seed into the ground; ²⁷ And should sleep, and rise night and day, and the seed should spring and grow up, he knoweth not how. ²⁸ For the earth bringeth forth fruit of herself; first the blade, then the ear, after that the full corn in the ear. ²⁹ But when the fruit is brought forth, immediately he putteth in the sickle, because the harvest is come" (Mark 4:26-29).

38) " ²⁵ Therefore I say unto you, Take no thought for your life, what ye shall eat, or what ye shall drink; nor yet for your body, what ye shall put on. Is not the life more than meat, and the body than raiment? ²⁶ Behold the fowls of the air: for they sow not, neither do they reap, nor gather into barns; yet your heavenly Father feedeth them. Are ye not much better than they? ²⁷ Which of you by taking thought can add one cubit unto his stature? ²⁸ And why take ye thought for raiment? Consider the lilies of the field, how they grow; they toil not, neither do they spin: ²⁹ And yet I say unto you, That even Solomon in all his glory was not arrayed like one of these. ³⁰ Wherefore, if God so clothe the grass of the field, which to day is, and to morrow is cast into the oven, shall he not much more clothe you, O ye of little faith?

[31] Therefore take no thought, saying, What shall we eat? or, What shall we drink? or, Wherewithal shall we be clothed? [32] (For after all these things do the Gentiles seek:) for your heavenly Father knoweth that ye have need of all these things. [33] But seek ye first the kingdom of God, and his righteousness; and all these things shall be added unto you. [34] Take therefore no thought for the morrow: for the morrow shall take thought for the things of itself. Sufficient unto the day is the evil thereof" (Matthew 6:25-34).

39) "[19] Then came the disciples to Jesus apart, and said, Why could not we cast him out? [20] And Jesus said unto them, Because of your unbelief: for verily I say unto you, If ye have faith as a grain of mustard seed, ye shall say unto this mountain, Remove hence to yonder place; and it shall remove; and nothing shall be impossible unto you" (Matthew 17:19-20).

40) " [4] And he answered and said unto them, Have ye not read, that he which made them at the beginning made them male and female, [5] And said, For this cause shall a man leave father and mother, and shall cleave to his wife: and they twain shall be one flesh? [6] Wherefore they are no more twain, but one flesh. What therefore God hath joined together, let not man put asunder" (Matthew 19:4-6).

Chapter 4: Hearts & Minds

1) "[6] Howbeit we speak wisdom among them that are perfect: yet not the wisdom of this world, nor of the princes of this world, that come to nought: [7] But we speak the wisdom of God in a mystery, even the hidden wisdom, which God ordained before the world unto our glory: [8] Which none of the princes of this world knew: for had they known it, they would not have crucified the Lord of glory. [9] But as it is written, Eye hath not seen, nor ear heard, neither have entered into the heart of man, the things which God hath prepared for them that love him. [10] But God hath revealed them unto us by his Spirit: for the Spirit searcheth all things, yea, the deep things of God. [11] For what man knoweth the things of a man, save the spirit of man which

is in him? even so the things of God knoweth no man, but the Spirit of God" (1 Corinthians 2:6-11).
2) "The thought of foolishness is sin: and the scorner is an abomination to men" (Proverbs 24:9).
3) "The wise man's eyes are in his head; but the fool walketh in darkness: and I myself perceived also that one event happeneth to them all" (Ecclesiastes 2:14).
4) "Through wisdom is an house builded; and by understanding it is established" (Proverbs 24:3).
5) "But they that will be rich fall into temptation and a snare, and into many foolish and hurtful lusts, which drown men in destruction and perdition" (1 Timothy 6:9).
6) " ⁶ And Elihu the son of Barachel the Buzite answered and said, I am young, and ye are very old; wherefore I was afraid, and durst not shew you mine opinion. ⁷ I said, Days should speak, and multitude of years should teach wisdom. ⁸ But there is a spirit in man: and the inspiration of the Almighty giveth them understanding. ⁹ Great men are not always wise: neither do the aged understand judgment" (Job 32:6-9).
7) "¹ When Ephraim spake trembling, he exalted himself in Israel; but when he offended in Baal, he died. ² And now they sin more and more, and have made them molten images of their silver, and idols according to their own understanding, all of it the work of the craftsmen: they say of them, Let the men that sacrifice kiss the calves. ³ Therefore they shall be as the morning cloud, and as the early dew that passeth away, as the chaff that is driven with the whirlwind out of the floor, and as the smoke out of the chimney" (Hosea 13:1-3).
8) "The adversaries of the LORD shall be broken to pieces; out of heaven shall he thunder upon them: the LORD shall judge the ends of the earth; and he shall give strength unto his king, and exalt the horn of his anointed" (1 Samuel 2:10).
9) "⁴ For there are certain men crept in unawares, who were before of old ordained to this condemnation, ungodly men, turning the grace of our God into lasciviousness, and denying the only Lord God, and our Lord Jesus Christ. ⁵ I will therefore put you in remembrance, though ye once knew this, how that the Lord, having saved the people out

of the land of Egypt, afterward destroyed them that believed not. [6] And the angels which kept not their first estate, but left their own habitation, he hath reserved in everlasting chains under darkness unto the judgment of the great day. [7] Even as Sodom and Gomorrha, and the cities about them in like manner, giving themselves over to fornication, and going after strange flesh, are set forth for an example, suffering the vengeance of eternal fire" (Jude 4-7).

10) "For in much wisdom is much grief: and he that increaseth knowledge increaseth sorrow" (Ecclesiastes 1:18).

11) " [8] And unto the angel of the church in Smyrna write; These things saith the first and the last, which was dead, and is alive; [9] I know thy works, and tribulation, and poverty, (but thou art rich) and I know the blasphemy of them which say they are Jews, and are not, but are the synagogue of Satan" (Revelation 2:8-9).

12) "[21] And if thou say in thine heart, How shall we know the word which the LORD hath not spoken? [22] When a prophet speaketh in the name of the LORD, if the thing follow not, nor come to pass, that is the thing which the LORD hath not spoken, but the prophet hath spoken it presumptuously: thou shalt not be afraid of him" (Deuteronomy 18:21-22).

13) "[43] For a good tree bringeth not forth corrupt fruit; neither doth a corrupt tree bring forth good fruit. [44] For every tree is known by his own fruit. For of thorns men do not gather figs, nor of a bramble bush gather they grapes. [45] A good man out of the good treasure of his heart bringeth forth that which is good; and an evil man out of the evil treasure of his heart bringeth forth that which is evil: for of the abundance of the heart his mouth speaketh" (Luke 6:43-45).

14) "A prudent man concealeth knowledge: but the heart of fools proclaimeth foolishness" (Proverbs 12:23).

15) "And the Spirit of God came upon Zechariah the son of Jehoiada the priest, which stood above the people, and said unto them, Thus saith God, Why transgress ye the commandments of the LORD, that ye cannot prosper? because ye have forsaken the LORD, he hath also forsaken you" (2 Chronicles 24:20).

16) " [19] What say I then? that the idol is any thing, or that which is offered in sacrifice to idols is any thing? [20] But I say, that the things which the

Gentiles sacrifice, they sacrifice to devils, and not to God: and I would not that ye should have fellowship with devils. [21] Ye cannot drink the cup of the Lord, and the cup of devils: ye cannot be partakers of the Lord's table, and of the table of devils" (1 Corinthians 10:19-21).

17) "Surely the serpent will bite without enchantment; and a babbler is no better" (Ecclesiastes 10:11).

18) "A lying tongue hateth those that are afflicted by it; and a flattering mouth worketh ruin" (Proverbs 26:28).

19) "Don't you see that the whole aim of Newspeak is to narrow the range of thought? In the end we shall make thoughtcrime literally impossible, because there will be no words in which to express it. Every concept that can ever be needed will be expressed by exactly one word, with its meaning rigidly defined and all its subsidiary meanings rubbed out and forgotten." George Orwell, Page 46 *1984,* Plume, Copyright © Harcourt Brace and Company, 1949.

20) "Speak not in the ears of a fool: for he will despise the wisdom of thy words" (Proverbs 23:9).

21) "[31] Then said Jesus to those Jews which believed on him, If ye continue in my word, then are ye my disciples indeed; [32] And ye shall know the truth, and the truth shall make you free" (John 8:31-32).

22) "[1] Now as touching things offered unto idols, we know that we all have knowledge. Knowledge puffeth up, but charity edifieth. [2] And if any man think that he knoweth anything, he knoweth nothing yet as he ought to know" (1 Corinthians 8:1-2).

23) "The wicked walk on every side, when the vilest men are exalted" (Psalm 12:8).

24) "Then said I, Wisdom is better than strength: nevertheless the poor man's wisdom is despised, and his words are not heard" (Ecclesiastes 9:16).

25) "[18] And Jesus came and spake unto them, saying, All power is given unto me in heaven and in earth. [19] Go ye therefore, and teach all nations, baptizing them in the name of the Father, and of the Son, and of the Holy Ghost: [20] Teaching them to observe all things whatsoever I have commanded you: and, lo, I am with you alway, even unto the end of the world. Amen" (Matthew 28:18-20).

26) [34] Jesus saith unto them, My meat is to do the will of him that sent me, and to finish his work. [35] Say not ye, There are yet four months, and

then cometh harvest? behold, I say unto you, Lift up your eyes, and look on the fields; for they are white already to harvest. [36] And he that reapeth receiveth wages, and gathereth fruit unto life eternal: that both he that soweth and he that reapeth may rejoice together. [37] And herein is that saying true, One soweth, and another reapeth. [38] I sent you to reap that whereon ye bestowed no labour: other men laboured, and ye are entered into their labours" John 4:34-38).

27) "A merry heart maketh a cheerful countenance: but by sorrow of the heart the spirit is broken" (Proverbs 15:13).

28) "A merry heart doeth good like a medicine: but a broken spirit drieth the bones" (Proverbs 17:22).

Chapter 5: Science & Philosophy

1) "Through faith we understand that the worlds were framed by the word of God, so that things which are seen were not made of things which do appear" (Hebrews 11:3).

2) "[19] Because that which may be known of God is manifest in them; for God hath shewed it unto them. [20] For the invisible things of him from the creation of the world are clearly seen, being understood by the things that are made, even his eternal power and Godhead; so that they are without excuse" (Romans 1:19-20).

3) "Evolution is not unquestionable fact." Justices Rehnquist & Scalia, 1987 United States Supreme Court Case (Edwards v. Aguilard), Page 25.

4) "The history of most fossil species includes two features particularly inconsistent with gradualism: 1.) Stasis. Most species exhibit no directional change during their tenure on earth. They appear in the fossil record looking much the same as when they disappear; Morphological change is usually limited and directionless. 2.) Sudden Appearance. In any local area, a species does not arise gradually by the steady transformation of its ancestors; it appears all at once and 'fully formed.'" Stephen J. Gould, "Evolution's Erratic Pace," *Natural History* 86 (1977): 13-14.

"What is missing are the many intermediate forms hypothesized by Darwin." Robert B. Carroll, curator of vertebrate paleontology at the Redpath

Museum at McGill University, ("Towards a New Evolutionary Synthesis," *Trends in Ecology and Evolution* 15[2000]: 27-32).

5) " [24] And God said, Let the earth bring forth the living creature after his kind, cattle, and creeping thing, and beast of the earth after his kind: and it was so. [25] And God made the beast of the earth after his kind, and cattle after their kind, and every thing that creepeth upon the earth after his kind: and God saw that it was good" (Genesis 1:24-25).

6) "Changes resulting from one or more of these factors have led to the extinction of most of the species of animals and plants that have inhabited the earth; in fact, of all the species that have existed in the course of the earth's history, only a tiny fraction remain alive today." Steven M. Stanley, Page 144, *Earth And Life Through Time*, Copyright © 1986, 1989 by W. H. Freeman and Company.

7) "In fact, the late Julian Huxley, once a leader among Darwinists, admitted that sexual freedom is a popular motivation behind evolutionary dogma. When he was asked by talk show host Merv Griffin, 'Why do people believe in evolution?' Huxley honestly answered, 'The reason we accepted Darwinism even without proof, is because we didn't want God to interfere with our sexual mores.'" quote from *I Don't Have Enough Faith To Be An Atheist*, page 163, Norman L. Geisler and Frank Turek, Crossway Books, 2004.

8) " [9] The thing that hath been, it is that which shall be; and that which is done is that which shall be done: and there is no new thing under the sun. [10] Is there any thing whereof it may be said, See, this is new? it hath been already of old time, which was before us" (Ecclesiastes 1:9-10).

9) "Absolute, true, and mathematical time, of itself, and from its own nature flows equably without regard to anything external, and by another name is called duration: relative, apparent, and common time, is some sensible and external (whether accurate or unequable) measure of duration by the means of motion, which is commonly used instead of true time; such as an hour, a day, a month, a year. Absolute space, in its own nature, without regard to anything external, remains always similar and immovable. Relative space is some movable dimension or measure of the absolute spaces; which our senses determine by its position to bodies; and which is vulgarly taken for immovable

space; such is the dimension of a subterraneous, an aerial, or celestial space, determined by its position in respect of the earth. Absolute and relative space are the same in figure and magnitude; but they do not remain always numerically the same. For if the earth, for instance, moves, a space of our air, which relatively and in respect of the earth remains always the same, will at one time be one part of the absolute space into which the air passes; at another time it will be another part of the same, and so, absolutely understood, it will be perpetually mutable." Isaac Newton translated by Andrew Motte, Pages 13 & 14, *The Principia*, Prometheus Books, 1995.

10) "[25] Of old hast thou laid the foundation of the earth: and the heavens are the work of thy hands. [26] They shall perish, but thou shalt endure: yea, all of them shall wax old like a garment; as a vesture shalt thou change them, and they shall be changed" (Psalm 102:25-26).

11) "[1] And I saw a new heaven and a new earth: for the first heaven and the first earth were passed away; and there was no more sea. [2] And I John saw the holy city, new Jerusalem, coming down from God out of heaven, prepared as a bride adorned for her husband. [3] And I heard a great voice out of heaven saying, Behold, the tabernacle of God is with men, and he will dwell with them, and they shall be his people, and God himself shall be with them, and be their God. [4] And God shall wipe away all tears from their eyes; and there shall be no more death, neither sorrow, nor crying, neither shall there be any more pain: for the former things are passed away. [5] And he that sat upon the throne said, Behold, I make all things new. And he said unto me, Write: for these words are true and faithful" (Revelation 21:1-5).

Chapter 6: Evil, Suffering, & Judgment

1) "I know, and am persuaded by the Lord Jesus, that there is nothing unclean of itself: but to him that esteemeth any thing to be unclean, to him it is unclean" (Romans 14:14).

2) "For meat destroy not the work of God. All things indeed are pure; but it is evil for that man who eateth with offence" (Romans 14:20).

3) "When the wicked spring as the grass, and when all the workers of iniquity do flourish; it is that they shall be destroyed for ever" (Psalm 92:7).

4) "[1] Woe is me! for I am as when they have gathered the summer fruits, as the grapegleanings of the vintage: there is no cluster to eat: my soul desired the firstripe fruit. [2] The good man is perished out of the earth: and there is none upright among men: they all lie in wait for blood; they hunt every man his brother with a net. [3] That they may do evil with both hands earnestly, the prince asketh, and the judge asketh for a reward; and the great man, he uttereth his mischievous desire: so they wrap it up. [4] The best of them is as a brier: the most upright is sharper than a thorn hedge: the day of thy watchmen and thy visitation cometh; now shall be their perplexity. [5] Trust ye not in a friend, put ye not confidence in a guide: keep the doors of thy mouth from her that lieth in thy bosom. [6] For the son dishonoureth the father, the daughter riseth up against her mother, the daughter in law against her mother in law; a man's enemies are the men of his own house" (Micah 7:1-6).

5) "The wicked shall be turned into hell, and all the nations that forget God" (Psalm 9:17).

6) "[12] Therefore rejoice, ye heavens, and ye that dwell in them. Woe to the inhabiters of the earth and of the sea! for the devil is come down unto you, having great wrath, because he knoweth that he hath but a short time. [13] And when the dragon saw that he was cast unto the earth, he persecuted the woman which brought forth the man child. [14] And to the woman were given two wings of a great eagle, that she might fly into the wilderness, into her place, where she is nourished for a time, and times, and half a time, from the face of the serpent. [15] And the serpent cast out of his mouth water as a flood after the woman, that he might cause her to be carried away of the flood. [16] And the earth helped the woman, and the earth opened her mouth, and swallowed up the flood which the dragon cast out of his mouth. [17] And the dragon was wroth with the woman, and went to make war with the remnant of her seed, which keep the commandments of God, and have the testimony of Jesus Christ" (Revelation 12:12-17).

7) "Because sentence against an evil work is not executed speedily, therefore the heart of the sons of men is fully set in them to do evil" (Ecclesiastes 8:11).

8) "But without faith it is impossible to please him: for he that cometh to God must believe that he is, and that he is a rewarder of them that diligently seek him" (Hebrews 11:6).

9) "Behold, I have created the smith that bloweth the coals in the fire, and that bringeth forth an instrument for his work; and I have created the waster to destroy" (Isaiah 54:16).

10) "[17] Now then it is no more I that do it, but sin that dwelleth in me. [18] For I know that in me (that is, in my flesh,) dwelleth no good thing: for to will is present with me; but how to perform that which is good I find not. [19] For the good that I would I do not: but the evil which I would not, that I do. [20] Now if I do that I would not, it is no more I that do it, but sin that dwelleth in me. [21] I find then a law, that, when I would do good, evil is present with me. [22] For I delight in the law of God after the inward man: [23] But I see another law in my members, warring against the law of my mind, and bringing me into captivity to the law of sin which is in my members" (Romans 7:17-23).

11) "[17] Do not ye yet understand, that whatsoever entereth in at the mouth goeth into the belly, and is cast out into the draught? [18] But those things which proceed out of the mouth come forth from the heart; and they defile the man. [19] For out of the heart proceed evil thoughts, murders, adulteries, fornications, thefts, false witness, blasphemies: [20] These are the things which defile a man: but to eat with unwashen hands defileth not a man" (Matthew 15:17-20).

12) "[1] And after these things I saw four angels standing on the four corners of the earth, holding the four winds of the earth, that the wind should not blow on the earth, nor on the sea, nor on any tree. [2] And I saw another angel ascending from the east, having the seal of the living God: and he cried with a loud voice to the four angels, to whom it was given to hurt the earth and the sea, [3] Saying, Hurt not the earth, neither the sea, nor the trees, till we have sealed the servants of our God in their foreheads" (Revelation 7:1-3).

13) "And God saw every thing that he had made, and, behold, it was very good. And the evening and the morning were the sixth day" (Genesis 1:31).
14) "The earth also is defiled under the inhabitants thereof; because they have transgressed the laws, changed the ordinance, broken the everlasting covenant" (Isaiah 24:5).
15) "Wherefore, as by one man sin entered into the world, and death by sin; and so death passed upon all men, for that all have sinned" (Romans 5:12).
16) "[3] Know ye not, that so many of us as were baptized into Jesus Christ were baptized into his death? [4] Therefore we are buried with him by baptism into death: that like as Christ was raised up from the dead by the glory of the Father, even so we also should walk in newness of life. [5] For if we have been planted together in the likeness of his death, we shall be also in the likeness of his resurrection: [6] Knowing this, that our old man is crucified with him, that the body of sin might be destroyed, that henceforth we should not serve sin. [7] For he that is dead is freed from sin" (Romans 6:3-7).
17) "[22] And the LORD God said, Behold, the man is become as one of us, to know good and evil: and now, lest he put forth his hand, and take also of the tree of life, and eat, and live for ever: [23] Therefore the LORD God sent him forth from the garden of Eden, to till the ground from whence he was taken. [24] So he drove out the man; and he placed at the east of the garden of Eden Cherubims, and a flaming sword which turned every way, to keep the way of the tree of life" (Genesis 3:22-24).
18) "He that committeth sin is of the devil; for the devil sinneth from the beginning. For this purpose the Son of God was manifested, that he might destroy the works of the devil" (1 John 3:8).
19) "And the devil that deceived them was cast into the lake of fire and brimstone, where the beast and the false prophet are, and shall be tormented day and night for ever and ever" (Revelation 20:10).
20) "Therefore rejoice, ye heavens, and ye that dwell in them. Woe to the inhabiters of the earth and of the sea! for the devil is come down unto you, having great wrath, because he knoweth that he hath but a short time" (Revelation 12:12).

21) "⁵ And Jehoshaphat stood in the congregation of Judah and Jerusalem, in the house of the LORD, before the new court, ⁶ And said, O LORD God of our fathers, art not thou God in heaven? and rulest not thou over all the kingdoms of the heathen? and in thine hand is there not power and might, so that none is able to withstand thee" (2 Chronicles 20:5-6)?
22) "Be sober, be vigilant; because your adversary the devil, as a roaring lion, walketh about, seeking whom he may devour" (1 Peter 5:8).
23) "¹ Now the serpent was more subtil than any beast of the field which the LORD God had made. And he said unto the woman, Yea, hath God said, Ye shall not eat of every tree of the garden? ² And the woman said unto the serpent, We may eat of the fruit of the trees of the garden: ³ But of the fruit of the tree which is in the midst of the garden, God hath said, Ye shall not eat of it, neither shall ye touch it, lest ye die. ⁴ And the serpent said unto the woman, Ye shall not surely die: ⁵ For God doth know that in the day ye eat thereof, then your eyes shall be opened, and ye shall be as gods, knowing good and evil. ⁶ And when the woman saw that the tree was good for food, and that it was pleasant to the eyes, and a tree to be desired to make one wise, she took of the fruit thereof, and did eat, and gave also unto her husband with her; and he did eat" (Genesis 3:1-6).
24) "¹³ For such are false apostles, deceitful workers, transforming themselves into the apostles of Christ. ¹⁴ And no marvel; for Satan himself is transformed into an angel of light" (2 Corinthians 11:13-14).
25) "Submit yourselves therefore to God. Resist the devil, and he will flee from you" (James 4:7).
26) "We know that whosoever is born of God sinneth not; but he that is begotten of God keepeth himself, and that wicked one toucheth him not" (1 John 5:18).
27) "Thou believest that there is one God; thou doest well: the devils also believe, and tremble" (James 2:19).
28) "⁶ They lavish gold out of the bag, and weigh silver in the balance, and hire a goldsmith; and he maketh it a god: they fall down, yea, they worship. ⁷ They bear him upon the shoulder, they carry him, and set him in his place, and he standeth; from his place shall he not remove:

yea, one shall cry unto him, yet can he not answer, nor save him out of his trouble" (Isaiah 46:6-7).

29) "Who is a liar but he that denieth that Jesus is the Christ? He is antichrist, that denieth the Father and the Son" (1 John 2:22).

30) "³² And they were astonished at his doctrine: for his word was with power. ³³ And in the synagogue there was a man, which had a spirit of an unclean devil, and cried out with a loud voice, ³⁴ Saying, Let us alone; what have we to do with thee, thou Jesus of Nazareth? art thou come to destroy us? I know thee who thou art; the Holy One of God" (Luke 4:32-34).

31) "¹ Hear the word of the LORD, ye children of Israel: for the LORD hath a controversy with the inhabitants of the land, because there is no truth, nor mercy, nor knowledge of God in the land. ² By swearing, and lying, and killing, and stealing, and committing adultery, they break out, and blood toucheth blood. ³ Therefore shall the land mourn, and every one that dwelleth therein shall languish, with the beasts of the field, and with the fowls of heaven; yea, the fishes of the sea also shall be taken away. ⁴ Yet let no man strive, nor reprove another: for thy people are as they that strive with the priest. ⁵ Therefore shalt thou fall in the day, and the prophet also shall fall with thee in the night, and I will destroy thy mother. ⁶ My people are destroyed for lack of knowledge: because thou hast rejected knowledge, I will also reject thee, that thou shalt be no priest to me: seeing thou hast forgotten the law of thy God, I will also forget thy children" (Hosea 4:1-6).

32) "³⁶ But I say unto you, That every idle word that men shall speak, they shall give account thereof in the day of judgment. ³⁷ For by thy words thou shalt be justified, and by thy words thou shalt be condemned" (Matthew 12:36-37).

33) "⁴⁶ I am come a light into the world, that whosoever believeth on me should not abide in darkness. ⁴⁷ And if any man hear my words, and believe not, I judge him not: for I came not to judge the world, but to save the world. ⁴⁸ He that rejecteth me, and receiveth not my words, hath one that judgeth him: the word that I have spoken, the same shall judge him in the last day" (John 12:46-48).

34) "Behold, I was shapen in iniquity; and in sin did my mother conceive me" (Psalm 51:5).

35) "He that hath an ear, let him hear what the Spirit saith unto the churches; He that overcometh shall not be hurt of the second death" (Revelation 2:11).

36) "[21] And the twelve gates were twelve pearls; every several gate was of one pearl: and the street of the city was pure gold, as it were transparent glass. [22] And I saw no temple therein: for the Lord God Almighty and the Lamb are the temple of it. [23] And the city had no need of the sun, neither of the moon, to shine in it: for the glory of God did lighten it, and the Lamb is the light thereof. [24] And the nations of them which are saved shall walk in the light of it: and the kings of the earth do bring their glory and honour into it. [25] And the gates of it shall not be shut at all by day: for there shall be no night there. [26] And they shall bring the glory and honour of the nations into it. [27] And there shall in no wise enter into it any thing that defileth, neither whatsoever worketh abomination, or maketh a lie: but they which are written in the Lamb's book of life" (Revelation 21:21-27).

37) "[1] But of the times and the seasons, brethren, ye have no need that I write unto you. [2] For yourselves know perfectly that the day of the Lord so cometh as a thief in the night. [3] For when they shall say, Peace and safety; then sudden destruction cometh upon them, as travail upon a woman with child; and they shall not escape. [4] But ye, brethren, are not in darkness, that that day should overtake you as a thief. [5] Ye are all the children of light, and the children of the day: we are not of the night, nor of darkness. [6] Therefore let us not sleep, as do others; but let us watch and be sober. [7] For they that sleep sleep in the night; and they that be drunken are drunken in the night. [8] But let us, who are of the day, be sober, putting on the breastplate of faith and love; and for an helmet, the hope of salvation. [9] For God hath not appointed us to wrath, but to obtain salvation by our Lord Jesus Christ, [10] Who died for us, that, whether we wake or sleep, we should live together with him" (1 Thessalonians 5:1-10).

38) "[17] For God sent not his Son into the world to condemn the world; but that the world through him might be saved. [18] He that believeth on him is not condemned: but he that believeth not is condemned already, because he hath not believed in the name of the only begotten Son of God" (John 3:17-18).

39) "To him that overcometh will I grant to sit with me in my throne, even as I also overcame, and am set down with my Father in his throne" (Revelation 3:21).
40) "Behold, all souls are mine; as the soul of the father, so also the soul of the son is mine: the soul that sinneth, it shall die" (Ezekiel 18:4).
41) "[23] For all have sinned, and come short of the glory of God; [24] Being justified freely by his grace through the redemption that is in Christ Jesus: [25] Whom God hath set forth to be a propitiation through faith in his blood, to declare his righteousness for the remission of sins that are past, through the forbearance of God" (Romans 3:23-25).
42) "[28] And we know that all things work together for good to them that love God, to them who are the called according to his purpose. [29] For whom he did foreknow, he also did predestinate to be conformed to the image of his Son, that he might be the firstborn among many brethren" (Romans 8:28-29).
43) "[38] Ye have heard that it hath been said, An eye for an eye, and a tooth for a tooth: [39] But I say unto you, That ye resist not evil: but whosoever shall smite thee on thy right cheek, turn to him the other also. [40] And if any man will sue thee at the law, and take away thy coat, let him have thy cloke also. [41] And whosoever shall compel thee to go a mile, go with him twain. [42] Give to him that asketh thee, and from him that would borrow of thee turn not thou away" (Matthew 5:38-42).
44) "[1] And the LORD spake unto Moses, saying, [2] Again, thou shalt say to the children of Israel, Whosoever he be of the children of Israel, or of the strangers that sojourn in Israel, that giveth any of his seed unto Molech; he shall surely be put to death: the people of the land shall stone him with stones. [3] And I will set my face against that man, and will cut him off from among his people; because he hath given of his seed unto Molech, to defile my sanctuary, and to profane my holy name. [4] And if the people of the land do any ways hide their eyes from the man, when he giveth of his seed unto Molech, and kill him not: [5] Then I will set my face against that man, and against his family, and will cut him off, and all that go a whoring after him, to commit whoredom with Molech, from among their people" (Leviticus 20:1-5).

45) "[17] Recompense to no man evil for evil. Provide things honest in the sight of all men. [18] If it be possible, as much as lieth in you, live peaceably with all men. [19] Dearly beloved, avenge not yourselves, but rather give place unto wrath: for it is written, Vengeance is mine; I will repay, saith the Lord. [20] Therefore if thine enemy hunger, feed him; if he thirst, give him drink: for in so doing thou shalt heap coals of fire on his head. [21] Be not overcome of evil, but overcome evil with good" (Romans 12:17-21).

Chapter 7: Economics

1) "An inheritance may be gotten hastily at the beginning; but the end thereof shall not be blessed" (Proverbs 20:21).
2) "He that hasteth to be rich hath an evil eye, and considereth not that poverty shall come upon him" (Proverbs 28:22).
3) " [23] Be thou diligent to know the state of thy flocks, and look well to thy herds. [24] For riches are not for ever: and doth the crown endure to every generation" (Proverbs 27:23-24)?
4) "Hell and destruction are never full; so the eyes of man are never satisfied" (Proverbs 27:20).
5) "He that loveth silver shall not be satisfied with silver; nor he that loveth abundance with increase: this is also vanity" (Ecclesiastes 5:10).
6) "As the partridge sitteth on eggs, and hatcheth them not; so he that getteth riches, and not by right, shall leave them in the midst of his days, and at his end shall be a fool" (Jeremiah 17:11).
7) "Except the LORD build the house, they labour in vain that build it: except the LORD keep the city, the watchman waketh but in vain" (Psalm 127:1).
8) "Treasures of wickedness profit nothing: but righteousness delivereth from death" (Proverbs 10:2).
9) "A good man leaveth an inheritance to his children's children: and the wealth of the sinner is laid up for the just" (Proverbs 13:22).
10) "[10] According to the grace of God which is given unto me, as a wise masterbuilder, I have laid the foundation, and another buildeth thereon. But let every man take heed how he buildeth thereupon. [11] For other

foundation can no man lay than that is laid, which is Jesus Christ" (1 Corinthians 3:10-11).

11) "Let not him that is deceived trust in vanity: for vanity shall be his recompence" (Job 15:31).

12) "…led by an invisible hand to promote an end which was no part of his intention. Nor is it always the worse for the society that it was no part of it. By pursuing his own interest he frequently promotes that of the society more effectually than when he really intends to promote it." Adam Smith, Page 572, The Wealth of Nations, originally published in 1776, this edition is based on the fifth edition as edited and annotated by Edwin Cannan in 1904, Bantam Classic Edition/ March 2003.

13) " [17] Even so every good tree bringeth forth good fruit; but a corrupt tree bringeth forth evil fruit. [18] A good tree cannot bring forth evil fruit, neither can a corrupt tree bring forth good fruit" (Matthew 7:17-18).

14) "For the love of money is the root of all evil: which while some coveted after, they have erred from the faith, and pierced themselves through with many sorrows" (1 Timothy 6:10).

15) "[31] Therefore take no thought, saying, What shall we eat? or, What shall we drink? or, Wherewithal shall we be clothed? [32] (For after all these things do the Gentiles seek:) for your heavenly Father knoweth that ye have need of all these things" (Matthew 6:31-32).

16) "The sleep of a labouring man is sweet, whether he eat little or much: but the abundance of the rich will not suffer him to sleep" (Ecclesiastes 5:12).

17) "When goods increase, they are increased that eat them: and what good is there to the owners thereof, saving the beholding of them with their eyes" (Ecclesiastes 5:11)?

18) "But Peter said unto him, Thy money perish with thee, because thou hast thought that the gift of God may be purchased with money" (Acts 8:20).

19) "[9] The fear of the LORD is clean, enduring for ever: the judgments of the LORD are true and righteous altogether. [10] More to be desired are they than gold, yea, than much fine gold: sweeter also than honey and the honeycomb" (Psalm 19:9-10).

20) "But he that knew not, and did commit things worthy of stripes, shall be beaten with few stripes. For unto whomsoever much is given, of him shall be much required: and to whom men have committed much, of him they will ask the more" (Luke 12:48).

Chapter 8: Law, Government, & Civics

1) "[1] And the whole earth was of one language, and of one speech. [2] And it came to pass, as they journeyed from the east, that they found a plain in the land of Shinar; and they dwelt there. [3] And they said one to another, Go to, let us make brick, and burn them throughly. And they had brick for stone, and slime had they for morter. [4] And they said, Go to, let us build us a city and a tower, whose top may reach unto heaven; and let us make us a name, lest we be scattered abroad upon the face of the whole earth. [5] And the LORD came down to see the city and the tower, which the children of men builded. [6] And the LORD said, Behold, the people is one, and they have all one language; and this they begin to do: and now nothing will be restrained from them, which they have imagined to do. [7] Go to, let us go down, and there confound their language, that they may not understand one another's speech. [8] So the LORD scattered them abroad from thence upon the face of all the earth: and they left off to build the city. [9] Therefore is the name of it called Babel; because the LORD did there confound the language of all the earth: and from thence did the LORD scatter them abroad upon the face of all the earth" (Genesis 11:1-9).
2) "And the LORD said, Behold, the people is one, and they have all one language; and this they begin to do: and now nothing will be restrained from them, which they have imagined to do" (Genesis 11:6).
3) "[12] How art thou fallen from heaven, O Lucifer, son of the morning! how art thou cut down to the ground, which didst weaken the nations! [13] For thou hast said in thine heart, I will ascend into heaven, I will exalt my throne above the stars of God: I will sit also upon the mount of the congregation, in the sides of the north: [14] I will

ascend above the heights of the clouds; I will be like the most High" (Isaiah 14:12-14).

4) "[1] But of the times and the seasons, brethren, ye have no need that I write unto you. [2] For yourselves know perfectly that the day of the Lord so cometh as a thief in the night. [3] For when they shall say, Peace and safety; then sudden destruction cometh upon them, as travail upon a woman with child; and they shall not escape" (1 Thessalonians 5:1-3).

5) " [3] The wicked are estranged from the womb: they go astray as soon as they be born, speaking lies. [4] Their poison is like the poison of a serpent: they are like the deaf adder that stoppeth her ear; [5] Which will not hearken to the voice of charmers, charming never so wisely" (Psalms 58:3-5).

6) "The most foolish mistake we could possibly make would be to allow the subjected people to carry arms; history shows that all conquerors who have allowed their subjected people to carry arms have prepared their own fall." Adolf Hitler, from *Edict of March 18, 1938*.

7) "[4] Then all the elders of Israel gathered themselves together, and came to Samuel unto Ramah, [5] And said unto him, Behold, thou art old, and thy sons walk not in thy ways: now make us a king to judge us like all the nations. [6] But the thing displeased Samuel, when they said, Give us a king to judge us. And Samuel prayed unto the LORD. [7] And the LORD said unto Samuel, Hearken unto the voice of the people in all that they say unto thee: for they have not rejected thee, but they have rejected me, that I should not reign over them. [8] According to all the works which they have done since the day that I brought them up out of Egypt even unto this day, wherewith they have forsaken me, and served other gods, so do they also unto thee. [9] Now therefore hearken unto their voice: howbeit yet protest solemnly unto them, and shew them the manner of the king that shall reign over them. [10] And Samuel told all the words of the LORD unto the people that asked of him a king. [11] And he said, This will be the manner of the king that shall reign over you: He will take your sons, and appoint them for himself, for his chariots, and to be his horsemen; and some shall run before his chariots. [12] And he will appoint him captains over thousands, and captains over fifties; and will set them to ear his

ground, and to reap his harvest, and to make his instruments of war, and instruments of his chariots. [13] And he will take your daughters to be confectionaries, and to be cooks, and to be bakers. [14] And he will take your fields, and your vineyards, and your oliveyards, even the best of them, and give them to his servants. [15] And he will take the tenth of your seed, and of your vineyards, and give to his officers, and to his servants. [16] And he will take your menservants, and your maidservants, and your goodliest young men, and your asses, and put them to his work. [17] He will take the tenth of your sheep: and ye shall be his servants.

[18] And ye shall cry out in that day because of your king which ye shall have chosen you; and the LORD will not hear you in that day" (1 Samuel 8:4-18).

8) "The affectionate sentiments of esteem and approbation which you are so good as to express towards me, on behalf of the Danbury Baptist association, give me the highest satisfaction. My duties dictate a faithful and zealous pursuit of the interests of my constituents, & in proportion as they are persuaded of my fidelity to those duties, the discharge of them becomes more and more pleasing. Believing with you that religion is a matter which lies solely between Man & his God, that he owes account to none other for his faith or his worship, that the legitimate powers of government reach actions only, & not opinions, I contemplate with sovereign reverence that act of the whole American people which declared that their legislature should "make no law respecting an establishment of religion, or prohibiting the free exercise thereof," thus building a wall of separation between Church & State. Adhering to this expression of the supreme will of the nation in behalf of the rights of conscience, I shall see with sincere satisfaction the progress of those sentiments which tend to restore to man all his natural rights, convinced he has no natural right in opposition to his social duties. I reciprocate your kind prayers for the protection & blessing of the common father and creator of man, and tender you for yourselves & your religious association, assurances of my high respect & esteem." Thomas Jefferson to a committee of the Danbury Baptist association in the state of Connecticut, January 1, 1802.

9) "Congress shall make no law respecting an establishment of religion, or prohibiting the free exercise thereof;" Amendment I. to the United States Constitution, ratified December 15th, 1791.

10) "Therefore the law is slacked, and judgment doth never go forth: for the wicked doth compass about the righteous; therefore wrong judgment proceedeth" (Habakkuk 1:4).

11) "Thou shalt not wrest judgment; thou shalt not respect persons, neither take a gift: for a gift doth blind the eyes of the wise, and pervert the words of the righteous" (Deuteronomy 16:19).

12) "To have respect of persons is not good: for for a piece of bread that man will transgress" (Proverbs 28:21).

13) "Let every soul be subject unto the higher powers. For there is no power but of God: the powers that be are ordained of God" (Romans 13:1).

14) " [22] And thou his son, O Belshazzar, hast not humbled thine heart, though thou knewest all this; [23] But hast lifted up thyself against the LORD of heaven; and they have brought the vessels of his house before thee, and thou, and thy lords, thy wives, and thy concubines, have drunk wine in them; and thou hast praised the gods of silver, and gold, of brass, iron, wood, and stone, which see not, nor hear, nor know: and the God in whose hand thy breath is, and whose are all thy ways, hast thou not glorified: [24] Then was the part of the hand sent from him; and this writing was written. [25] And this is the writing that was written, MENE, MENE, TEKEL, UPHARSIN. [26] This is the interpretation of the thing: MENE; God hath numbered thy kingdom, and finished it. [27] TEKEL; Thou art weighed in the balances, and art found wanting. [28] PERES; Thy kingdom is divided, and given to the Medes and Persians. [29] Then commanded Belshazzar, and they clothed Daniel with scarlet, and put a chain of gold about his neck, and made a proclamation concerning him, that he should be the third ruler in the kingdom. [30] In that night was Belshazzar the king of the Chaldeans slain. [31] And Darius the Median took the kingdom, being about threescore and two years old" (Daniel 5:22-31).

15) "[14] I am the good shepherd, and know my sheep, and am known of mine. [15] As the Father knoweth me, even so know I the Father: and I lay down my life for the sheep. [16] And other sheep I have, which are not

of this fold: them also I must bring, and they shall hear my voice; and there shall be one fold, and one shepherd" (John 10:14-16).

16) "[1] Let every soul be subject unto the higher powers. For there is no power but of God: the powers that be are ordained of God. [2] Whosoever therefore resisteth the power, resisteth the ordinance of God: and they that resist shall receive to themselves damnation. [3] For rulers are not a terror to good works, but to the evil. Wilt thou then not be afraid of the power? do that which is good, and thou shalt have praise of the same: [4] For he is the minister of God to thee for good. But if thou do that which is evil, be afraid; for he beareth not the sword in vain: for he is the minister of God, a revenger to execute wrath upon him that doeth evil. [5] Wherefore ye must needs be subject, not only for wrath, but also for conscience sake. [6] For for this cause pay ye tribute also: for they are God's ministers, attending continually upon this very thing. [7] Render therefore to all their dues: tribute to whom tribute is due; custom to whom custom; fear to whom fear; honour to whom honour" (Romans 13:1-7).

17) " [28] Saying, Did not we straitly command you that ye should not teach in this name? and, behold, ye have filled Jerusalem with your doctrine, and intend to bring this man's blood upon us. [29] Then Peter and the other apostles answered and said, We ought to obey God rather than men" (Acts 5:28-29).

18) "[13] Submit yourselves to every ordinance of man for the Lord's sake: whether it be to the king, as supreme; [14] Or unto governors, as unto them that are sent by him for the punishment of evildoers, and for the praise of them that do well" (1 Peter 2:13-14).

19) " [5] And now go to; I will tell you what I will do to my vineyard: I will take away the hedge thereof, and it shall be eaten up; and break down the wall thereof, and it shall be trodden down: [6] And I will lay it waste: it shall not be pruned, nor digged; but there shall come up briers and thorns: I will also command the clouds that they rain no rain upon it" (Isaiah 5:5-6).

20) "A man that flattereth his neighbour spreadeth a net for his feet" (Proverbs 29:5).

21) "The king by judgment establisheth the land: but he that receiveth gifts overthroweth it" (Proverbs 29:4).

22) " [16] And they sent out unto him their disciples with the Herodians, saying, Master, we know that thou art true, and teachest the way of God in truth, neither carest thou for any man: for thou regardest not the person of men. [17] Tell us therefore, What thinkest thou? Is it lawful to give tribute unto Caesar, or not? [18] But Jesus perceived their wickedness, and said, Why tempt ye me, ye hypocrites? [19] Shew me the tribute money. And they brought unto him a penny. [20] And he saith unto them, Whose is this image and superscription? [21] They say unto him, Caesar's. Then saith he unto them, Render therefore unto Caesar the things which are Caesar's; and unto God the things that are God's" (Matthew 22:16-21).

23) "[26] Be ye angry, and sin not: let not the sun go down upon your wrath: [27] Neither give place to the devil" (Ephesians 4:26-27).

24) "And concerning the tithe of the herd, or of the flock, even of whatsoever passeth under the rod, the tenth shall be holy unto the LORD" (Leviticus 27:32).

25) "[14] And unto the angel of the church of the Laodiceans write; These things saith the Amen, the faithful and true witness, the beginning of the creation of God; [15] I know thy works, that thou art neither cold nor hot: I would thou wert cold or hot. [16] So then because thou art lukewarm, and neither cold nor hot, I will spue thee out of my mouth" (Revelation 3:14-16).

26) "[6] For the punishment of the iniquity of the daughter of my people is greater than the punishment of the sin of Sodom, that was overthrown as in a moment, and no hands stayed on her. [7] Her Nazarites were purer than snow, they were whiter than milk, they were more ruddy in body than rubies, their polishing was of sapphire: [8] Their visage is blacker than a coal; they are not known in the streets: their skin cleaveth to their bones; it is withered, it is become like a stick. [9] They that be slain with the sword are better than they that be slain with hunger: for these pine away, stricken through for want of the fruits of the field" (Lamentations 4:6-9).

Section B: Glossary of Terms

Terms used and defined in the glossary are *italicized* for the reader.

A

Abaddon – king of the locusts, the angel of the bottomless pit mentioned in Revelation 9:11; also known as Apollyon (a destroyer)

Abraham – Abram, son of Terah, father of Isaac and Ishmael, the patriarch of Israel and father of many nations

Activism – doctrine or practice encouraging direct participation in mass demonstrations in support or opposition to one side of an issue

Adaptations – modifications to organisms that help them survive in the conditions of their environment

Age of Reason – 17th century Western world philosophy generally regarded as the beginning of modern philosophy; Deistic pamphlet written by Thomas Paine published in three parts (1794, 1795, and 1807) that criticizes institutionalized religion and challenges the legitimacy of the Bible

Agency – person or thing through which power is exerted

Agnostics – people who believe any ultimate reality (such as God) is unknown and probably unknowable

Alchemy – power or process used to transform something ordinary into something special: inexplicable transmutation

Alien Astronaut Theory – theory that extraterrestrials visited earth in the past and seeded life on the planet

Altruism – unselfish regard for or selfless devotion to the welfare of others

Anarchy – state of lawlessness or political disorder due to absence of government

Anomalies – deviations from the common rule, abnormal things that are not easily classified

Anthropic Principle – principle derived from the many necessary and precise interdependent cosmological and terrestrial variables, which make human life possible on planet earth: evidence for design

Apathy – lack of feeling or emotion, or lack of interest or concern: indifference

Apostasy – abandonment or renunciation of previous religious faith

Apostates – those who commit apostasy: See Apostasy.

Apple Of His Eye – the people of God, the nation of Israel (Deuteronomy 32:9-10)

Ascendancy – governing or controlling influence

Atheism – doctrine that holds the belief there is no deity

Atheists – people who deny the existence of God

Atheocracies – states governed by atheism

Autocracy – government where one person possesses unlimited power

Automatons – individuals who act in a mechanical fashion

Autonomy – quality or state of being self-governing

B

Backsliders – people who lapse morally or in the practice of religion

Balkanize – to break up into smaller and often more hostile groups

Barbarism – social or intellectual condition lacking restraint

Barriers to Entry – obstacles in the path of a firm that impedes or prevents it from entering a given market

Beachhead – area on a hostile shore occupied in order to secure further landing troops and provisions

Benchmark – point of reference from which a measurement can be made; something that serves as a standard

Bibbery – addiction to drinking

Big Bang – theory that the universe originated from a single mass explosion billions of years ago

Bigots – persons obstinately or intolerantly devoted to their own opinions and prejudices

Bigotry – acts or beliefs characteristic of bigots: See Bigots.

Blight – something which impairs or destroys; something that frustrates others' plans or hopes

Blighted – affected with blight: See Blight.

Blogs – (combination of the term web logs) websites or parts of websites usually maintained by individuals with regular commentaries or other materials such as video or graphics

Body of His Son – the eternal church, the body of believers in Christ Jesus (1 Corinthians 12:12-27)

Book of Life – book which contains the names of God's servants (Philippians 4:3)

Bootlickers – people who try to gain favor by being servile or obsequious

Booty – rich gain or prize: spoil

Botulism – an acute food poisoning caused by botulin contained in foods

Brain Stem – part of the brain made up by the mesencephalon, pons, and medulla oblongata that is connected to the spinal cord with the forebrain and cerebrum

Branch of Jesse – prophesied offspring of David who shall grow out of His roots; King of Israel the Gentiles shall seek (Isaiah 11:1-16): See Messiah.

Buckler – small round shield held by a handle at arm's length

Bulwarks – solid, wall-like structures erected for defense

Bureaucrats – government officials who follow formal rigid routines, or who have great authority in their own department

C

Caesar – emperor of Rome, ruling authority to whom tribute is due (Matthew 22:16-21)

Cafeteria Morality – cafeteria-style morality in which people pick and choose which doctrines to follow

Cambrian Explosion – abrupt appearance of nearly all major known animal groups in full form in Cambrian strata (believed to be between 500 and 600 million years ago)

Capitalism – economic system characterized by private or corporate ownership of capital goods that works by investment and competition in a free market place

Carnality – quality, state, or degree of being fleshly, or given over to crude bodily pleasures or appetites

Carrion – dead, putrefying flesh unfit for food

Case Law – reported court decisions which can be used to make interpretations of law: precedent law

Centrists – people who hold moderate views

Chaff – something that is comparatively worthless

Christian/Christians – one(s) who profess(es) belief in the teachings of Jesus Christ, or anything of or relating to Christianity: See Christianity.

Christianity – religion derived from Jesus Christ, based on the Bible

Churls – medieval peasants; rude ill-bred persons, or persons with sullen attitudes

Collateral Damage – damage unintended or incidental to the intended outcome

Collectivism – political or economic theory that advocates collective control, or a system marked by control

Communism – system in which a single dictatorial party controls the means of production with the aim of producing a stateless society

Communist/Communists – adherent(s) or advocate(s) of communism: See Communism.

Confederates – persons allied together for unlawful purposes

Constructionists – people who construe legal documents in a specific way

Consumerism – preoccupation with and an inclination toward the buying of consumer goods

Corpulence – the state of being excessively fat

Creation – See Creationism.

Creationism – doctrine that states that matter, the universe, and all life was created by God out of nothing

Crony capitalism – capitalist economy in which success in business depends on relationships between individuals in private business and government officials

Cupidity – strong or inordinate desire for wealth

D

Darwinism – evolution, the theory life evolved through natural selection; doctrine espousing the claims of Charles Darwin: See Theory of Evolution.

Dead in Christ – those dead to the world who will be resurrected like Christ (Romans 8:10-11)

Dearth – scarcity or inadequate supply that makes dear: famine

Deicide – act of killing a divine being or a symbol of such a being

Demagogues – leaders who exploit popular prejudices in order to gain power

Democracy/Democracies – government(s) ruled by the people through a system of majority rule

Despot/Despots – ruler(s) with absolute authority and power, or one(s) who abuse(s) power oppressively or tyrannically

Detritus – loose material that directly results from disintegration

Divine Predestination – that which has been determined beforehand by God

Divine Providence – care or guidance by God

E

Earled – past tense of to become an earl

Egalitarianism – social philosophy which advocates the removal of inequalities among people

Empathy – action of understanding, being aware of, being sensitive to, and vicariously experiencing others' feelings or thoughts without having the feelings or thoughts fully communicated in an objectively explicit manner

Empirical – capable of being proved or disproved either by observation or experimentation

Enlightenment – 18th century philosophical movement that rejected traditional social, religious, and political norms and emphasized rationalism

Entropy – second law of thermodynamics; measurement of disorder of a closed system, quantity for determining the direction which all natural processes go

Equilibrium – a state of balance

Ethos – distinguishing character, moral nature, or guiding beliefs of a person, group, or institution

Eugenicists – students or advocates of eugenics: See Eugenics.

Eugenics – science that deals with the improvement of heredity primarily by controlling human breeding

Euthanasia – act of killing or allowing the death of individuals who are hopelessly sick or injured for mercy's sake

Evolution – See Theory of Evolution.

Evolutionists – proponents or teachers of evolution: See Theory of Evolution.

Existentialism – 20th century philosophy embracing diversity and centering on the belief there are no right or wrongs or absolutes

Existentialists – adherents of existentialism: See Existentialism.

Extremism – quality or state of being extreme

Eye for an Eye – Old Testament law illustrated in Exodus 21:18-36, Exodus 22:1-15, Leviticus 24:18-21, Numbers 5:5-8, and Deuteronomy 19:15-21

F

Fabianism – slow rather than revolutionary change in government; doctrine of the Fabian Society organized in England in 1884

Fallen Angel – See Lucifer.

Fallow – to plow, harrow, and break up land without seeding to destroy weeds and conserve moisture: prepare soil for future harvest

Feces – bodily waste discharged through the anus

Federal – formed by a compact between political units that surrender their individual sovereignty to a centralized authority but retain limited residuary powers of government

Fetter – something which confines

Feudal – of, relating to, or suggestive of feudalism

Feudal Fief – estate in which a lord imposes a fee or homage upon tenants

Feudal lord – lord under feudalism

Fossils – persons whose views are outdated

Fundamentalists – supporters of movements stressing strict and literal adherence to a set of basic principles

G

Gaffes – diplomatic or social blunders: Faux pas

Gentile – person of a non-Jewish nation or of non-Jewish faith: Heathen

Godhead – God's nature, the three persons of God (Romans 1:20): See Trinity.

Gospel – the message concerning Christ, the kingdom of God, and salvation

Government Ownership – property interests vested in the state rather than individuals or communities

Great White Throne – the place of final judgment (Revelation 20:11-15)

H

Hedonists – practitioners of hedonism; people who embrace the doctrine that pleasure or happiness is the sole or chief good in life

Heisenberg Uncertainty Principle – principle in science named after physicist Karl Heisenberg that says it is impossible to determine with perfect accuracy the position and momentum of a particle at any given point in time

Hellions – troublesome or mischievous persons

Hire – payment for labor or services: wages

Hot LZ – (short for hot landing zone) a term used to describe a landing zone under enemy fire

Humanism – doctrine centered on human values, which rejects the supernatural and embraces reason

Humanists – persons devoted to humanism: See Humanism.

I

Id – one part of the three divisions of the psyche in psychoanalytic theory that is completely unconscious; source of instinctual needs and drives

Idioms – distinct languages peculiar to a certain people, community, or class

Idolatry – the worship of physical objects as gods, or the manufacturing of a god

Idols – false gods

Immutability – immutableness, capability of not being susceptible to change

Imp – a small demon or mischievous child: fiend

Imperialism – policy or practice of one nation extending its authority over others by imposing power and influence either through direct territorial acquisition or indirect control of the political and economic process

Inking – the act of drawing or writing on in ink

Intelligence – information concerning enemies or possible enemies or areas

Irreducible Complexity – system composed of interacting matched parts that together form a basic function, wherein removal of any part results in a complete failure of the entire system

Ivan Pavlov's Dogs – dogs used by Ivan Pavlov during his 1889 classical reflex conditioning experiment in St. Petersburg, Russia

Ivory Tower – aloof attitude marked by a lack of concern for the urgent or practical matters

J

Jettison – voluntary sacrifice of cargo to lighten a ship's load during times of difficulty

Jew/Jews – Israelite(s): person(s) belonging to a continuation through descent or conversion of the ancient Jewish people

K

Karl Marx and Friedrich Engels – socialist writers of "The Communist Manifesto" published in 1848

Kinetic Energy – energies associated with the motion of material bodies and subsequent forces

King of kings and Lord of lords – title for Jesus Christ (Revelation 19:11-16)

Knavery – rogue or mischievous acts

Know – term used in the English Bible for sexual intercourse

L

Laid – past and past part of lay, as in laying sexually with another person

Laissez-Faire – doctrine which opposes governmental intervention in economic affairs beyond what is necessary

Lake of Fire – place of final judgment reserved for death, hell, and those not found in the book of life: the second death (Revelation 20:13-15)

Lampreys – aquatic vertebrates of the order Hyperoartia that are widely distributed in temperate and subarctic regions in both fresh and salt water and resemble eels but have a large suctorial mouth

Lavatories – toilets

Lawgiver – The Lord (Isaiah 33:22)

Logistics – the handling of the details of an operation, or an aspect of military science dealing with the procurement, maintenance, and transportation of military materiel, facilities, and personnel

Lucifer – the devil, the fallen one cast from heaven, or Luciferian Babylon (Isaiah 14:12-15): See Satan.

M

Macroevolution – evolution on a large scale; any evolutionary change at or above the level of species

Malcontents – people who bear grudges from a sense of grievance or thwarted ambition: discontented people

Mammon – material possessions or wealth: worldly goods

Marxism – political, economic, and social principles espoused by Karl Marx, including the labor theory of value, dialectical materialism, the class struggle, and dictatorship of the proletariat until the establishment of a classless society: socialism

Marxist/Marxists – adherent(s) or advocate(s) of Marxism: See Marxism.

Messiah – King and Deliverer of Israel (Daniel 9:25-26): the Anointed One

Metaphysics – philosophical examination, a study of what lies beyond objective experience

Metastasize – to spread through transfer of disease-producing agency from the site of disease to another part of the body

Mete - boundary

Microevolution – evolution on a small scale; any evolutionary change below the level of species

Mirth – gladness shown by or accompanied with laughter: glee

Miser – individual who lives a miserable existence in order to hoard wealth

Monarchies – nations or states ruled by a single person

Monoculturalism – doctrine or theory of anything monocultural

Monolithic – something characterized as exhibiting rigid or fixed uniformity

Moral Entropy – steady degradation of a moral system or society: See Entropy.

Multiculturalism – doctrine or theory of anything multicultural

Multiple Universe Theory – term coined in 1895 by philosopher and psychologist William James to describe a hypothetical set of universes within a multiverse

N

Narcissists – egocentric individuals

Natural Selection – primary mechanism believed for evolution; selection process based on heritable variability resulting from differences in longevity and reproduction rates of progeny: survival of the fittest

Naturalism – doctrine that states all phenomena can be explained through scientific laws: nature is all there is

Naturalists – people who practice or advocate naturalism: See naturalism.

Nature – creative and controlling force in the universe

New Age Religion – decentralized social and spiritual movement in the West that seeks to attain the highest individual human potential through enlightenment and "Universal Truth"

New Testament – last twenty-seven books of the Christian Bible, consisting of the four canonized Gospels, the Epistles, the book of Acts, and Revelation

New World Order – vision of the world where greater peace and stability is achieved through a new political order

Nietzsche – Friedrich Wilhelm, German philosopher who said God is dead

Nimrod – mighty Hamitic hunter who became the king of Babel (Genesis 10:8-10)

Noisome – offensive to the senses, particularly to the sense of smell: noxious or unwholesome

Norms – typical behavior patterns or traits of a social group

O

Occult – actions or influences of supernatural powers or a hidden knowledge of them

Old Age Religion – the doctrines of devils: See Paganism.

Old Testament – first thirty-nine books of the Christian Bible, made up of canonized Jewish scripture: the Hebrew Bible

Oligarchies – governments in which a small group of individuals exercises control

Opulence – wealth, affluence, or abundance

P

Pacifism – opposition to war and violence as a means to settle conflict, or an attitude or policy of nonresistance

Paganism – polytheistic religions of ancient cultures, which center on sensuality, materialism, and hedonism

Pariah – member of a low caste: outcast

Pews – benches fixed in rows in a church with backs and sometimes doors

Phoenix – person or thing likened to the legendary bird that burned itself to ashes on a pyre and then rose alive from the ashes to live for another period

Phylums – groups with unity, primary divisions of the animal kingdom

Platitudes – banal, trite, or stale remarks

Pluralistic – of or relating to the theory there is more than one kind of supreme reality

Police States – political units which are characterized by repressive governmental control of political, economic, and social life, usually existing by an arbitrary exercise of power by police and especially secret police in place of regular operation of administrative and judicial organs of the government according to publicly known legal procedures

Political Correctness – term that denotes language, ideas, policies, or behaviors that are seen as seeking to minimize social and institutional offense in issues such as occupation, gender, race, culture, sexual orientation, disability, and age

Political Spin – form of propaganda achieved through providing interpretations of events or campaigns in order to persuade public opinion in favor of or against certain organizations or public figures

Ponzi Schemes – investment swindles in which early investors are paid with money supplied by later investors in order to encourage bigger and more risks

Pork – (as in pork barrel) government project or appropriation that yields benefits to a political district and its representative

Potential Energy – the energy a piece of matter has due to its position or because of how its parts are arranged

Primordial Ooze – theoretical liquid rich in organic compounds favorable for producing and growing life forms

Progressives – anyone who believes political and social changes come through governmental action

Prophet – title for Jesus Christ (John 7:37-40)

Propitiation – the act of or something that conciliates or gains or regains favor

PSYOPS – (short for psychological operations) planned operations to convey selected information with the sole purpose of influencing the emotions, motives, objective reasoning, and behavior of targeted groups and individuals

Purchasing Power – extent to which a person, firm, or group has available funds to make purchases

ρ

Quickened – those made alive

R

Rationalism – theory that reason is in itself a source of knowledge and is independent of and superior to sense perceptions

Redeemer – title for Jesus Christ (Revelation 5:9)

Relativism – theory that knowledge is relative to limited human understanding; the belief that ethical truths depend on the individual

Relativists – adherents of relativism: See relativism.

Representative Democracy – democracy where citizens delegate authority to elected representatives

Rock – title for Jesus Christ (1 Corinthians 10:1-4)

Rook – to defraud by cheating or swindling

Root of David – title for Jesus Christ (Revelation 22:16): See Branch of Jesse.

Rosetta Stone – basalt stone found in 1799 with hieroglyphic, demotic, and Greek inscriptions that helped decipher Egyptian hieroglyphics

Ruddiness – the state, condition, or quality of having a healthy reddish color

S

Sages – persons distinguished for wisdom and sound judgment

Satan – the devil, the accuser of the brethren (Revelation 12:7-10): See Lucifer.

Schisms — divisions, splits, gulfs, or rifts

Schizophrenia — the presence of mutually contradictory or antagonistic parts or qualities

Schizophrenic — characterized by schizophrenia: See Schizophrenia.

Scientism — methods and beliefs of natural scientists, faith-like reliance on the effectiveness of natural science to produce answers in an investigation

Secularism — indifference toward or a rejection or exclusion of religion and religious considerations

Secularists — advocates or practitioners of secularism: See Secularism.

Serf/Serfs — member(s) of the servile feudal class bound to the will of a lord

Sexual Revolution — 1960s and 1970s movement that sought to change social thought and attitudes toward sexuality and sexual behavior throughout the Western world

Shinar — plain where Noah's descendants built the tower of Babel in ancient times (Genesis 11:1-2)

Shofar — ram's horn trumpet blown by ancient Hebrews in battle and during religious observances

Silent Majority — term popularized in 1969 by Richard Nixon that means a large unspecified majority of a population who do not express public opinions

Singularities — things out of the ordinary, distinguished points

Section B: Glossary of Terms 231

Situational Ethics – system of ethics by which acts are judged within their contexts rather than by categorical principles

Sloth/Sloths – individual(s) disinclined to action or labor

Social Engineering – management of human beings in accordance with their place and role in society

Social Justice – early 20th century movement that tried to bring social order in agreement with Christian principles: social gospel

Socialism – any economic or political theory that advocates collective or governmental control over the means of production and distribution of goods

Socialist/Socialists – advocate(s) or practitioner(s) of socialism, or member(s) of a socialist group: See Socialism.

Sociopathic – anything related to or characterized by asocial or antisocial behavior or a psychopathic personality

Sorcery – use of power gained from the control or assistance of evil spirits: occult magic

Sound Bites – very short pieces of speech taken from a longer speech or interview considered to be the most important point, or brief statements by someone with authority for broadcasting

Speakeasies – places where alcoholic beverages are illegally sold

Specified Complexity – specific resident message contained within: example DNA

Stagflation – persistent inflation combined with stagnant consumer demand, resulting in high unemployment

Stasis – state of static balance or equilibrium

Statutory Law – statutes enacted by legislatures

Supply and Demand – economic model of price determination in a market where the unit price for a particular good varies until it settles at a point where the quantity demanded by consumers will equal the quantity supplied by producers, resulting in economic equilibrium of price and quantity

Surety – formal engagement (pledge) given to fulfill an undertaking

Sword – The Word of God (Ephesians 6:17): See Word of God.

T

Tender – anything offered in payment

The Origin of Species – book written by Charles Darwin and published in 1859 that introduced the scientific theory that populations evolve over time through a process called natural selection

Theory of Evolution – theory made popular by *The Origin of Species* written by Charles Darwin and published in 1859; theory based on the change in the inherited traits of a population of organisms through successive generations: See Darwinism.

Thrall – the state of a bondman or slave, or the act of enslaving

Transitional Forms – fossilized remains of intermediary life forms that demonstrate evolutionary transition: missing links

Tribalism – loyalty to a tribe above all other groups

Tribute – excessive tax or tariff imposed by a lord

Trinity – God; Father, Son, and Holy Spirit: See Godhead.

Tyranny – oppressive power

Tyranny of the Mob – democratic system in which decisions by a majority place the majority's interests so far above dissenters that dissenters become actively oppressed

U

Ungulates – hoofed animals that are mostly herbivorous

Uniformitarianism – doctrine in geology that assumes processes of the past are essentially the same as those of the present day

Usury – unconscionable or exorbitant rate of interest

Utilitarianism – doctrine which claims the useful is good and that right conduct should be determined by usefulness of its consequences

Utopias – places of ideal civic and social perfection

W

Whelp – one of the young of carnivorous mammals, or despised people or their offspring

Wicked One – the devil (Matthew 13:19)

Word of God – God's word contained in the Bible: Holy Scripture

WORD OF GOD – title for Jesus Christ (Revelation 19:11-13)

Wrested – pulled, forced, or moved by violent wringing movements: twisted

Y

Yoke/Yokes – wooden bar(s) or frame(s) by which two draft animals are joined together at the heads or necks for work, or oppressive agency/agencies

Youthful Idealism – practice of young people forming ideals or living under their influence, or something idealized by youth

Z

Zealotry – excessive zeal; fanatical devotion

For more information about
Brian Ridolfi
&
Useful Maxims
please visit:

facebook.com/BrianRidolfiAuthor

For more information about
AMBASSADOR INTERNATIONAL
please visit:

www.ambassador-international.com
@AmbassadorIntl
www.facebook.com/AmbassadorIntl